C0-ARK-471

MEDIUM AND MESSAGE IN JUDAISM
First Series

Number 179
MEDIUM AND MESSAGE IN JUDAISM
First Series

by
Jacob Neusner

MEDIUM AND MESSAGE IN JUDAISM

First Series

by

Jacob Neusner

Scholars Press
Atlanta, Georgia

MEDIUM AND MESSAGE IN JUDIASM
First Series

Library of Congress Cataloging in Publication Data

Neusner, Jacob, 1932-
  Medium and message in Judaism. First series / Jacob Neusner.
    p. cm. -- (Brown Judaic studies ; no. 179)
    Includes index.
    ISBN 1-55540-378-6
    1. Mishnah--Criticism, interpretation, etc. I. Title.
II. Series.
BM497.8.N4766   1989
296.1'2306--dc20   89-35718
                                        CIP

Printed in the United States of America
on acid-free paper

In memory of
Rafi Zaiman
on his ninth
Yahrzeit.

CONTENTS

Preface

In Part One I make the basic point of the book as a whole that there is a neat fit between the message that an authorship chooses and the literary medium that the same authorship selects for conveying that message. Chapter One asks about the interplay of rhetoric and logic in the Mishnah. My proposition is that these two components of the medium of a piece of writing, the one on the framing of thought, the other on the connections between one thought and another, serve admirably for the philosophical purposes of the authorship of the document. Then the medium and the message reciprocally sustain one another. The notion that the proposition is everything, the style nothing, is contradicted when we can show, as I do in Chapter Two, for example, that the particular message of both the Mishnah and Scripture turns out to correspond in an exact way to the particular media chosen by each, that is, rhetoric and logic of cogent discourse. The Scripture appeals to narrative and teleological logic, the Mishnah to the rhetoric of *Listenwissenschaft* and propositional, syllogistic logic, the one to convey a theological point for a tradition, the other, a philosophical point for a system. Here I find the match between medium and message exact because I discern in the medium the main points of the message.

Part Two turns to the relationship of the message and the medium, now with stress on the message that the medium conveys. By medium I mean three things, each covered in one of the papers before us. The first is literary medium, hence the account of the relationship of the Mishnah to Scripture. The second is intellectual medium, that is, mode of thought, and I describe the way in which the philosophers of the Mishnah identified and solved problems. The third is systemic medium, that is to say, the whole and encompassing message at hand; here the question is why a given systemic medium treats one topic rather than some other, and why we find in a given Judaism attention to issues, here economics, that another Judaism ignores. Chapter Three began as a lecture at the University of Florence on January 20, 1989.

Chapter Four summarizes in a brief way some fairly substantial work on the way in which a given mode of thought dictates the conclusions people reach and the problems they will wish to solve. Chapter Five asks why Judaism has an economics. It was presented as a lecture at the University of Bologna on January 19, 1989. I take this opportunity to thank my gracious hosts in Italy, in not only Florence and Bologna, but also two Vatican universities, Pontifical Lateran University and Pontifical Anselm University, the Protestant Theological Faculty of Rome, and also the Jewish Community of Turin.

Part Three consists of one paper. I ask how we ourselves receive the messages of the Mishnah, which is to say, the context in which we identify pertinent data and make sense of them. At stake is how the document conveys ideas. Modern and even contemporary scholarship, from the nineteenth century onward, brought to the document, in quest of an account of its ideas, the premises of our own day. People have therefore tended to assume that the messages of Judaism are cast into the medium of specific words, each one standing for a given idea. So words denote ideas. Therefore, if we know the right word, we can find all the passages containing the idea for which that word stands, that is, the messages for which that word serves as medium. Then by an account of all of those occurrences of that word and the sense of each passage, we assume that we know the idea for which that word stands.

That method misconstrues the medium by which the framers of the Mishnah (and other rabbinic writings) conducted discourse. Their medium did not resort to fixed and final meanings of given words, that is to say, through a single word-choice they did not say everything that they had to say about a given subject. Words connote and denote but do not exhaust conceptions. To the contrary, words prove only one medium, and not the main or most reliable one, by which we gain access to the messages of the rabbinic writings. This is the discovery and demonstration of Max Kadushin. I call attention in this paper to a demonstration of the fallacy of the opposite position that words guide us into concepts. It is the work of Howard Eilberg-Schwartz which began in my seminar as a study of two words and how they are used but ballooned into a book on *The Human Will in Judaism,* in which that same corpus of evidence served, and served all by itself, for a much vaster topic indeed.

In Part Four I turn to the messages that I think derive from the received media of a particular Judaism, the one that appeals to the Dual Torah. I set forth what that conception is supposed to mean. This shows us the mythic framing of a theological belief. We see how the teachings of sages are presented in the medium of "tradition," thereby endowing those teachings with an authority and a theological apologia that they would not otherwise have enjoyed.

The final section turns to the media for conveying religious messages in contemporary Judaism. Messages pass in both directions, from community to the realm of systematic thought, and from systematic thought to the community. In Chapter Nine, which is my lecture of January 10, 1989, at the Pontifical Anselm University at the Vatican, I ask what message is conveyed concerning Judaism by the conduct of Jews vis-à-vis Judaic liturgy. Specifically, I want to know what we learn about the power or pathos of the received Judaism of the Dual Torah from the willingness of large numbers of Jews to conform to its liturgical world in one way but not in another. In this case the contemporary message derives from the conduct of the faithful. From what they do, we learn the shape and structure of their faith. Our consideration of the media for conveying Judaic messages concludes in Chapter Ten with the use of history for theological discourse and argument. That sort of impoverished, unphilosophical, theological discussion is commonplace. It offers the advantage of appeal to tangible facts, facts of history, but the disadvantage of asking historical facts to settle questions to which those facts do not gain access at all, questions of religious faith for instance. In my review, originally printed in the *National Review*, of two current books of historistic and positivist theology, both by Jews and both addressing "the Holocaust," I point out the inappropriate premises and consequently the awry conclusions.

Part One
THE MEDIUM AND THE MESSAGE

1

The Mishnah's Match of Rhetoric and Logic

Prima facie evidence that the Mishnah is to be read as a philosophical writing derives from the character of the rhetoric and of the logic of the document. The rhetoric is propositional and, as I shall explain, syllogistic. One logic prevails, a paramount logic of cogent discourse that establishes propositions resting upon philosophical bases. This logic joins facts to one another to yield a proposition through the proposal of a thesis and the composition of a list of facts that (e.g., through shared traits of a taxonomic order) prove the thesis. So the rhetoric that predominates facilitates appeal to a logic that is propositional. The Mishnah's mode of making connections and drawing conclusions from them requires, specifically, a vast labor of classification, comparison, and contrast, generating governing rules and generalizations. The predominant rhetorical pattern exactly suits the accomplishment of that work. That is the basis for my claim that the rhetoric and the logic of the document powerfully facilitate the philosophical mission assigned to the writing by the philosophers who made the document.

Let us begin with the traits of rhetoric. If in detail most of the sixty-one tractates of the Mishnah are readily distinguished from Scripture, in general they conduct discourse in such a way that any relationship at all with a prior writing is, if not denied, then at least subordinated. And that fact draws us deeper into the intellectual world of the authorship of the document. For the bridge from proposition, *what* people think, to process, *how* they think, is built of modes of discourse. And the character of mishnaic discourse, as much as the content thereof, demonstrates the intent of the authorship. It was to speak inductively and descriptively, that is, philosophically, about propositions that yielded philosophy.

Concentrating on the facts of the tractate, as we did just now, misses the paramount and definitive traits of the document as a whole. The negative side contains a positive fact. The authorship has not appealed to Scripture for its modes of holding together distinct thoughts in a coherent statement; it does not frame its ideas as a commentary, let alone as an amplification of the sense and application of scriptural law. Other writings of the same Judaism did just that. But still more blatant, the difference between the Hebrew of Scripture and the Hebrew of the Mishnah more tellingly testifies to utter indifference concerning continuity with Scripture. Shifting language from scriptural and therefore archaic Hebrew, such as we find in the Essene writings of the Dead Sea, to an essentially new syntax and fresh morphology, such as we find in the Mishnah, requires us to focus attention upon the character of discourse, not only its non-scriptural or ascriptural contents.

To state matters simply, the syllogistic medium bears the philosophical message in a very obvious way. In Scripture, a narrative form joins with a teleological logic (terms spelled out in Chapter Two) to present cogent discourse. In the Mishnah, a philosophical form joins with propositional, specifically, syllogistic and taxonomic logic, to make possible cogent discourse. These are profoundly different modes of discourse indeed, each serving its own well-defined purpose in a well-crafted piece of writing or canon of such writings. Now to spell out the facts that bear out these characterizations of the Mishnah as a distinctive, and I claim particularly philosophical, mode of discourse.

In the Mishnah, there is only one paramount principle of cogent order, and that is defined by the requirements of the exposition of a topic and its indicative traits. Accordingly, one established criterion for the delineation of an aggregate of materials from some other aggregate, fore or aft, will be a shift in the theme, or predominant and characteristic concern, of a sequence of materials. For most tractates, as for Meilah, we can account for the layout of themes or problems, explain why the framers have treated a given problem within their topic before, or after, they addressed another problem within that same topic.

The second fundamental criterion is the literary character, the syntactical and grammatical pattern, which differentiates and characterizes a sequence of primitive (that is, undifferentiable, indivisible) units of thought. Normally, when the subject changes, the mode of expression, the formal or formulary character, the patterning of language, will change as well. Understanding how this formal-literary mode of cogent discourse works draws us deep into the orderly thought-patterns of this writing.

All of the rhetoric operative in the Mishnah is propositional. Where one pattern differs from another, it gives authors the opportunity to shift from form to form as the subject changes. But no rhetorical pattern within the document's repertoire will serve an other than syllogistic purpose. The authorship of the Mishnah manages to say whatever it wants in one of the following ways:

1. the simple declarative sentence, in which the subject, verb, and predicate are syntactically tightly joined to one another, e.g., he who does so and so is such and such;

2. the duplicated subject, in which the subject of the sentence is stated twice, e.g., he who does so and so, lo, he is such and such;

3. mild apocopation, in which the subject of the sentence is cut off from the verb, which refers to its own subject, and not the one with which the sentence commences, e.g., he who does so and so..., it [the thing he has done] is such and such;

4. extreme apocopation, in which a series of clauses is presented, none of them tightly joined to what precedes or follows, and all of them cut off from the predicate of the sentence, e.g., he who does so and so..., it [the thing he has done] is such and such..., it is a matter of doubt whether...or whether...lo, it [referring to nothing in the antecedent, apocopated clauses of the subject of the sentence] is so and so.

5. In addition to these formulary patterns, in which the distinctive formulary traits are effected through variations in the relationship between the subject and the predicate of the sentence, or in which the subject itself is given a distinctive development, there is yet a fifth. In this last one we have a contrastive complex predicate, in which case we may have two sentences, independent of one another, yet clearly formulated so as to stand in acute balance with one another in the predicate, thus, *He who does...is unclean, and he who does not...is clean.*

It naturally will be objected, is it possible that "a simple declarative sentence" may be asked to serve as a formulary pattern, alongside the rather distinctive and unusual constructions which follow? True, by itself, a tightly constructed sentence consisting of subject, verb, and complement, in which the verb refers to the subject and the complement to the verb, hardly exhibits traits of particular formal interest. Yet a sequence of such sentences, built along the same gross grammatical lines, may well exhibit a clear-cut and distinctive pattern.

The philosophical mode of discourse then emerges blatantly. The authorship wishes to generalize, but only through cases. In rhetoric, what this means is that, while the Mishnah is not a generalizing document, the authorship makes its points by repeating several cases that yield the same, ordinarily unarticulated, general principle. It does this by paying close attention to the number of times a given form is used to set forth a given case to make a single point. The authorship commonly utilizes sets of three or five repetitions of cases to make a single point. Now when we see that three or five "simple declarative sentences" take up one principle or problem, and then, when the principle or problem shifts, a quite distinctive formal pattern will be utilized, we realize that the "simple declarative sentence" has served the formulator of the unit of thought as aptly as did apocopation, a dispute, or another more obviously distinctive form or formal pattern. The contrastive predicate is one example; the Mishnah contains many more.

Why do I claim that this rhetoric of convention and repetition bears a peculiarly philosophical burden? Because of the formation of patterns around principles, which is to say, the focus of formal choices upon recurrence in the aggregate of what I called earlier "an intermediate cognitive unit," or what we would call "a paragraph." And, in context, that constitutes the syllogism established by a list of like entries. The important point of differentiation, particularly for the simple declarative sentence, makes its appearance in the intermediate cognitive unit, thus in the interplay between theme and form. It is there that we see a single pattern recurring in a long sequence of sentences, e.g., *the X which has lost its Y is unclean because of its Z. The Z which has lost its Y is unclean because of its X.* Another example will be a long sequence of highly developed sentences, laden with relative clauses and other explanatory matter, in which a single syntactical pattern will govern the articulation of three or six or nine exempla. That sequence will be followed by one repeated terse sentence pattern, e.g., *X is so and so, Y is such and such, Z is thus and so.* The former group will treat one principle or theme, the latter some other. There can be no doubt, therefore, that the declarative sentence in recurrent patterns is, in its way, just as carefully formalized as a sequence of severely apocopated sentences or of contrastive predicates or duplicated subjects. So much for what is important about the document's rhetoric, which is its obvious serviceability for the presentation of propositional thought of a syllogistic character.

Second in order of analysis is the logic of a document. I use the simple word, logic, to stand for the principle of intelligibility and cogency of thought and the expression of thought in public discourse.

Logic is what joins one sentence to the next and forms the whole into paragraphs of meaning, intelligible propositions, each with its place and sense in a still larger, accessible system. Because of logic one mind connects to another, public discourse becomes possible, debate on issues of general intelligibility takes place, and an *anthology* of statements about a single subject becomes a *composition* of theorems about that subject. What people think – exegesis in accord with a fixed hermeneutic of the system – knows no limit. How they think makes all the difference. And how they think explains to us the connections people make between one thing and something else.

Discourse shared by others begins when one sentence joins to a second one in framing a statement in such a way that others understand *the connection* between the two sentences. In the canon of the Judaism of the Dual Torah there are four different logics by which two or more sentences are deemed to cohere and so to constitute a statement of consequence and intelligibility. The four logics are philosophical propositional, teleological narrative, methodical analytical, and fixed associative. The philosophical-propositional and teleological-narrative logics present the two (to us familiar) modes of turning two sentences into a coherent statement, one weight and meaning. These both connect two or more sentences, forming them into a whole, and also present a statement that in meaning and intelligible proposition transcends the sum of the parts.

The first two require little exposition. One is familiar to us as philosophical logic, the second is equally familiar as the logic of cogent discourse attained through narrative. These two, self-evidently, are logics of a propositional order, evoking a logic of a philosophical character. They differ in that the former speaks plainly, the latter indirectly; the former appeals to the here and the now, the latter to the power of metaphor. But both logics say things, and coherence derives from what is said.

The third logic is not propositional. It is a logic of fixed association, in which the joining of two or more sentences into sizable conglomerates does not appeal to the sense of what is said, but the extrinsic framework in which what is said is located. The fourth mode of coherent discourse is equally unfamiliar, though it is more readily accessible. It is a mode of establishing connections at the most abstract level of thought through highly methodical analysis of many things in a single way. On the surface it also is not propositional, and it requires an active and engaged mind to draw forth the propositions that methodical-analytical thought yields. But through the reader's mind, this logic, too, does set forth its encompassing truths of order, proportion, structure, and self-evidence.

We must dwell on the first of the four kinds of logic because it not only is paramount, but it also forms a philosophical logic in a way the others do not. The first logic establishes propositions that rest upon philosophical bases, e.g., through the proposal of a thesis and the composition of a list of facts that prove the thesis. This is to us an entirely familiar, Western mode of scientific expression through the classification of data. It is the way of natural philosophy, yielding science. We may call it the science of – deriving from – making lists (*Listenwissenschaft*). This philosophical logic of cogent discourse works in a familiar way. It involves the rationality of putting two and two together to reach the conclusion of four.

That is to say, the generative issue is one of connection, not of fact but of the relationship between one fact and another. The two or more facts, that is, sentences, are connected through the conclusion, the syllogism that is supposed to derive from the connection. The conclusion or proposition is different from the established facts. When we set up as a sequence two or more facts and deduce from that sequence a proposition different from, and transcending, the facts at hand, we join the two sentences or facts in the philosophical logic of cogent discourse that is most common in our own setting. And this comprises the logic of propositional discourse. We demonstrate propositions in a variety of ways, appealing to both a repertoire of probative facts and also a set of accepted modes of argument. In this way we engage in a kind of discourse that gains its logic from what the rigorous analysis and testing of propositions against the canons of an accepted reason applied to analysis of pertinent evidence. It is philosophy that accomplishes the miracle of making the whole more than the sum of the parts, that is, in the simple language I have used up to now, showing the connections between fact 1 and fact 2 to yield proposition A.

The inner logic is readily described. The Mishnah's philosophers uncover rules by comparison and contrast, showing the rule for one thing by finding out how it compares with like things and contrasts with the unlike.[1] Then, in their view, the rule governing the unknown would become known, conforming as it did to the rule of the like thing, or it would prove the opposite of the rule governing the unlike thing. List-making places on display the data of the like and the unlike and therefore conveys the rule: like follows like, unlike follows the opposite rule. And that brings us back to the rhetorical traits of the writing, the composition of lists, distinguished syntactically as well as

---

[1]Compare G. E. R. Lloyd, *Polarity and Analogy. Two Types of Argumentation in Early Greek Thought* (Cambridge: Cambridge University Press, 1966). But the core-logic of *Listenwissenschaft* extends back to Sumerian times.

syllogistically from one another. To serve for philosophical purposes, the Mishnah had to be a book of lists, with the implicit order, the nomothetic traits, dictating the ordinarily unstated general and encompassing rule.

Listenwissenschaft joins rhetoric to logic in the search for the rule governing many things by classification of things by shared traits. The framers of the Mishnah in defining those taxonomic indicators that dictate what belongs on one list, what on some other, appeal solely to the intrinsic traits of things. *Listenwissenschaft* defines a way of proving propositions through classification, so establishing a set of shared traits that form a rule which compels us to reach a given conclusion. Probative facts derive from the classification of data, all of which point in one direction and not in another. And that defines philosophical method from Aristotle forward.

One pericope of the Mishnah suffices to show us the logic that joins fact to fact, sentence to sentence, in a cogent proposition, and, furthermore, to establish a syllogism that transcends the facts at hand: to create new knowledge. Our case involves the government of Israel, the Jewish people. There are in the philosophers' republic, twin sources of authority: king and high priest. How do these relate, and which is the more important? These questions, of course, signal the fundamental interest in hierarchization and show us how the system asks, and answers, its most urgent questions of hierarchical taxonomy: ordering of all things, each in its proper place. The high priest and king fall into a single genus, but speciation, based on traits particular to the king, then distinguishes the one from the other.[2]

In the following passage, drawn from Mishnah-tractate Sanhedrin Chapter Two, the authorship wishes to say that Israel has two heads, one of state, the other of cult, the king and the high priest, respectively, and that these two offices are nearly wholly congruent with one another with a few differences based on the particular traits of each. Broadly speaking, therefore, our exercise is one of setting forth the genus and the species. The genus is head of holy Israel. The species are king and high priest. Here are the traits in common and those not shared, and the exercise is fully exposed for what it is, an inquiry into the rules that govern, the points of regularity and order, in this minor

---

[2]We note once more that all of this exercise is conducted essentially independently of Scripture, even though Scripture does contribute irrefutable facts. The reason that Scripture is not generative is that the classifications derive from the system, are viewed as autonomous constructs; traits of things define classifications and dictate what is like and what is unlike. That underlines the point made in Chapter Four.

matter, of political structure. My outline, imposed in bold-face type, makes the point important in this setting.

Mishnah-tractate Sanhedrin Chapter Two

1. *The rules of the high priest: subject to the law, marital rites, conduct in bereavement*

2:1

A.   A high priest judges, and [others] judge him;

B.   gives testimony, and [others] give testimony about him;

C.   performs the rite of removing the shoe [Deut. 25:7-9], and [others] perform the rite of removing the shoe with his wife.

D.   [Others] enter levirate marriage with his wife, but he does not enter into levirate marriage,

E.   because he is prohibited to marry a widow.

F.   [If] he suffers a death [in his family], he does not follow the bier.

G.   "But when [the bearers of the bier] are not visible, he is visible; when they are visible, he is not.

H.   "And he goes with them to the city gate," the words of R. Meir.

I.   R. Judah says, "He never leaves the sanctuary,

J.   "since it says, 'Nor shall he go out of the sanctuary' (Lev. 21:12)."

K.   And when he gives comfort to others,

L.   the accepted practice is for all the people to pass one after another, and the appointed [prefect of the priests] stands between him and the people.

M.   And when he receives consolation from others,

N.   all the people say to him, "Let us be your atonement."

O.   And he says to them, "May you be blessed by Heaven."

P.   And when they provide him with the funeral meal,

Q.   all the people sit on the ground, while he sits on a stool.

2. *The rules of the king: not subject to the law, marital rites, conduct in bereavement*

2:2

A.   The king does not judge, and [others] do not judge him;

B.   does not give testimony, and [others] do not give testimony about him;

C.   does not perform the rite of removing the shoe, and others do not perform the rite of removing the shoe with his wife;

D.   does not enter into levirate marriage, nor [do his brothers] enter levirate marriage with his wife.

E.   R. Judah says, "If he wanted to perform the rite of removing the shoe or to enter into levirate marriage, his memory is a blessing."

F.   They said to him, "They pay no attention to him [if he expressed the wish to do so]."

G.   [Others] do not marry his widow.

H.   R. Judah says, "A king may marry the widow of a king.

I.   "For so we find in the case of David, that he married the widow of Saul,

J. "For it is said, 'And I gave you your master's house and your master's wives into your embrace' (2 Sam. 12:8)."

2:3

A. [If] [the king] suffers a death in his family, he does not leave the gate of his palace.

B. R. Judah says, "If he wants to go out after the bier, he goes out,

C. "for thus we find in the case of David, that he went out after the bier of Abner,

D. "since it is said, 'And King David followed the bier' (2 Sam. 3:31)."

E. They said to him, "This action was only to appease the people."

F. And when they provide him with the funeral meal, all the people sit on the ground, while he sits on a couch.

3. *Special rules pertinent to the king because of the intrinsic traits of his calling or of the scriptural rules that pertain*

2:4

A. [The king] calls out [the army to wage] a war fought by choice on the instructions of a court of seventy-one.

B. He [may exercise the right to] open a road for himself, and [others] may not stop him.

C. The royal road has no required measure.

D. All the people plunder and lay before him [what they have grabbed], and he takes the first portion.

E. "He should not multiply wives to himself" (Deut. 17:17) – only eighteen.

F. R. Judah says, "He may have as many as he wants, so long as they do not entice him [to abandon the Lord (Deut. 7:4)]."

G. R. Simeon says, "Even if there is only one who entices him [to abandon the Lord] – lo, this one should not marry her."

H. If so, why is it said, "He should not multiply wives to himself"?

I. Even though they should be like Abigail (1 Sam. 25:3).

J. "He should not multiply horses to himself" (Deut. 17:16) – only enough for his chariot.

K. "Neither shall he greatly multiply to himself silver and gold" (Deut. 17:16) – only enough to pay his army.

L. "And he writes out a scroll of the Torah for himself" (Deut. 17:17).

M. When he goes to war, he takes it out with him; when he comes back, he brings it back with him; when he is in session in court, it is with him; when he is reclining, it is before him,

N. as it is said, "And it shall be with him, and he shall read in it all the days of his life" (Deut. 17:19).

2:5

A. [Others may] not ride on his horse, sit on his throne, handle his sceptre.

B. And [others may] not watch him while he is getting a haircut, or while he is nude, or in the bath-house,

C. since it is said, "You shall surely set him as king over you" (Deut. 17:15) – that reverence for him will be upon you.

The philosophical cast of mind is amply revealed in this essay, which in concrete terms effects a taxonomy, a study of the genus, national leader, and its two species, [1] king, [2] high priest.[3] We ask, how are they alike, how are they not alike, and what accounts for the differences? The premise is that national leaders are alike and follow the same rule, except where they differ and follow the opposite rule from one another.

But that premise also is subject to the proof effected by the survey of the data consisting of concrete rules, those systemically inert facts that here come to life for the purposes of establishing a proposition. By itself, the fact that, e.g., others may not ride on his horse, bears the burden of no systemic proposition. In the context of an argument constructed for nomothetic, taxonomic purposes, the same fact is active and weighty. The whole depends upon three premises: [1] the importance of comparison and contrast, with the supposition that [2] like follows the like, and the unlike follows the opposite, rule; and [3] when we classify, we also hierarchize, which yields the argument from hierarchical classification: if this, which is the lesser, follows rule X, then that, which is the greater, surely should follow rule X. And that is the whole sum and substance of the logic of *Listenwissenschaft* as the Mishnah applies that logic in a practical way.

There is another logic suitable for philosophy that also comes into play, though not so commonly as *Listenwissenschaft* in the Mishnah, the logic of methodical analysis. Here one analytical method applies to many sentences with the result that many discrete and diverse sentences are shown to constitute a single intellectual structure. A variety of explanations and amplifications, topically and propositionally unrelated, will be joined in a methodical way so as to produce a broadly applicable conclusion that many things really conform to a single pattern or structure. Such methodologically coherent analysis imposes on a variety of data a structure that is external to all of the data, yet that imposes connection between and among facts or sentences. The connection consists in the recurrent order and repeated balance and replicated meaning of them all, seen in the aggregate. This is commonly done by asking the same question to many things and producing a single result many times. Unity of thought and discourse therefore derives not only from what is said, or even from a

---

[3]The subordination of Scripture to the classification scheme is self-evident. Scripture supplies facts. The traits of things – kings, high priests – dictate classification categories on their own, without Scripture's dictate.

set of fixed associations. In a profound sense, the Mishnah's discrete exercises of *Listenwissenschaft* find their ultimate coherence only in the repetition of the same method many times, and that yields a generalization not made explicit at any point, and yet ineluctable and blatant throughout.

Methodical analysis may be conducted by addressing a set of fixed questions, imposing a sequence of stable procedures, to a vast variety of data. That will yield not a proposition, nor even a sequence of facts formerly unconnected but now connected, but a different mode of cogency, one that derives from showing that many things follow a single rule or may be interpreted in a single way. It is the intelligible proposition that is general and not particular, that imposes upon the whole a sense of understanding and comprehension, even though the parts of the whole do not join together. This mode of discourse turns the particular into the general, the case into a rule.

Neither of the other two available logics, the teleological and the fixed associative, served in the Mishnah, though both appear in other writings of the Judaism of the Dual Torah. Teleological logic of cogent and intelligent discourse also sets forth propositions, but the propositions do not derive from the intrinsic traits of things. Their place in some larger plan, their purpose, their teleology are what hold facts together and make of them all a proposition that transcends the details. Narrative is the common rhetorical choice for teleological logic, and within the narrative the teleology serves to connect one sentence, fact, or thought to another. A proposition (whether or not it is stated explicitly) may be set forth and demonstrated by showing through the telling of a tale (of a variety of kinds, e.g., historical, fictional, parabolic, and the like) that a sequence of events, real or imagined, shows the ineluctable truth of a given proposition.

The logic of connection demonstrated through narrative, rather than philosophy, is simply stated. It is connection attained and explained by invoking some mode of narrative in which a sequence of events, first this, then that, is understood to yield a proposition, first this, then that *because of this.* That sequence both states and establishes a proposition in a way different from the philosophical and argumentative mode of propositional discourse. Whether or not the generalization is stated in so many words rarely matters because the power of well-crafted narrative is to make unnecessary explicit drawing of the moral.

Teleological logic, useless in the Mishnah, proved highly serviceable to the pentateuchal system because teleological logic rests upon the premise of an ineluctable union between the actions of persons and the events that affect the society they form. And that conception, in theology called covenantal, characterizes the fundamental cogency of thought, and, incidentally, also of discourse, in the Pentateuch. "If you do this, that will happen," forms a statement linking an action to a social and historical result, and that forms, in another dimension, a teleological connection as well. Thus: "If you walk in my statutes and observe my commandments and do them, then I will give you your rains in their season" (Lev. 26:3), "But if you will not hearken to me and will not do all these commandments, ...I will do this to you: I will appoint over you sudden terror...and you shall sow your seed in vain for your enemies shall eat it...Then the land shall enjoy its Sabbaths as long as it lies desolate while you are in your enemies' land...." (Lev. 26:34)

That teleology of connection and conclusion tells us what facts join what other facts, and what conclusions we are to draw in consequence. It is a uniform logic, and the structure of the pentateuchal intellect seems to me remarkably cogent. The claim of *purpose, therefore cause,* is presented in the garb of a story of what happened. Narrative conveys a proposition through the setting forth of happenings in a framework of inevitability, in a sequence that makes a point, e.g., establishes not merely the facts of what happens, but the teleology that explains those facts. Then we speak not only of events – our naked facts – but of their relationship. We claim to account for that relationship teleologically in the purposive sequence and necessary order of happenings.

The fourth logic in the canon of the Judaism that commences, after Scripture, with the Mishnah is the logic of fixed association. Here distinct facts or sentences or thoughts are held together without actually joining into sequential and coherent propositions of any kind. What we have in the logic of fixed association is a composition that sets forth a sequence of sentences that are, in content or inherent traits, absolutely unrelated. The composition is made up in each instance of a fixed sequence of words, e.g., a text, broken up into small units or clauses, e.g., a clause of a verse, and each of these fixedly associated units is followed by a phrase of amplification. The phrase pertains to the fixedly associated unit but not to anything else. That is to say, nothing links one sentence (completed thought) to the ones fore or aft. Yet the compositors have presented us with what they represent side by side with sentences that do form large compositions, that is, that are linked one to the next by connections that we can readily discern. That seems to me to indicate that our authorship conceives one mode of connecting sentences to form a counterpart to another. Fixed-associative logic is the exact opposite of propositional logic, whether philosophical and syllogistic or narrative and teleological.

How then does the logic of cogent discourse supplied by fixed association accomplish its goal? Rhetorically, we appeal to the commentary: citation of the base text, e.g., Scripture, followed by a few words of explanation or amplification. The rhetoric yields a sequence of sentences that bear no relationship or connection at all to one another. These discrete sentences appear in "commentary form," for instance:

"Clause 1": "this means A."
"Clause 2": "this refers to Q."

Nothing joins A and Q. Indeed, had I used symbols out of different classifications altogether, e.g., A, a letter of an alphabet, and a symbol such as #, which stands for something other than a sound of an alphabet, the picture would have proved still clearer. Nothing joins A to Q or A to # except that clause 2 follows clause 1. The upshot is that no proposition links A to Q or A to # and so far as there is a connection between A and Q or A and #, it is not propositional. Then is there a connection at all? I think the authorship of the document that set forth matters as they did assumes that there is such a connection. For there clearly is – at the very least – an order, that is, "clause 1" is prior to "clause 2," in the text that out of clauses 1 and 2 does form an intelligible statement, that is, two connected, not merely adjacent, sentences.

This mode of connection establishes intelligible discourse although it yields no proposition, no sense, no joining between two sentences, no implicit connection accessible without considerable labor of access. Even where there is no proposition at all, and even where the relationship between sentence A and sentence X does not derive from the interplay among the propositions at hand, facts are identified and connections are made. This logic is remote from our own world of thought, for it is very hard for us even to imagine (outside the realm of feeling or inchoate attitude) non-propositional and yet intelligible discourse. But it is a commonplace logic everywhere beyond the Mishnah. And in the writings of other Judaisms, including those prior to the Mishnah itself, it certainly makes its appearance, for example, in the Essene pesher-writings of the Dead Sea library. That is why I claim this logic, too, presented a choice and along with teleological logic demonstrates the null hypothesis.

In rhetorical form exegetical, remarkably suitable for a tradition deriving from a book deemed holy, this logic rests on a premise of a rationality that is inculcated through education in particular writings – that is, of prior discourse attained through processes of learning a logic not accessible, as are the logics of philosophy and narrative, but through another means. *The logic rests upon the premise that an established sequence of words joins whatever is attached to those words into a set of cogent statements, even though it does not form of those statements propositions of any kind, implicit or explicit.* T h e established sequence of words may be made up of names always associated with one another. It may be made up of a received text, with deep meanings of its own, e.g., a verse or a clause of Scripture. It may be made up of the sequence of holy days or synagogue lections, which are assumed to be known by everyone and so to connect on their own. The fixed association of these words, whether names, whether formulae such as verses of Scripture, whether lists of facts, serves to link otherwise unrelated statements to one another and to form of them all not a proposition but, nonetheless, *an entirely intelligible sequence of connected or related sentences.*

It remains to ask, do the rhetoric and the logic fit together in carrying out and even giving expression to the document's fundamental purpose and message? At stake in the answer is whether we may, on the surface, find in the document traits of system and philosophical order. In a well-crafted system, expressed in a fine piece of writing, rhetoric and logic carry out the tasks of the system-builders. Whether we explore the extrinsic traits of formal expression or the most profound layers of the logic of intelligible discourse and coherent thought that hold sentences together and form of them all propositions or presentations that can be understood, we produce a single result. It is that the well-crafted document's authorship does make choices in such a way as to work out a rationality of its own. Choosing modes of cogent discourse and coherent thought involves limiting thought within a repertoire that is exceedingly limited. So, too, within a quite diverse literary-rhetorical heritage, people select some few ways of saying a great many things.

The upshot of this account is to show the union of rhetoric and logic. Both serve a distinctively propositional mode of discourse. The mode of discourse facilitates syllogistic demonstration of propositions of a general character. We may now turn to the Mishnah's philosophy, because we understand the system's rhetoric and logic and can classify it as philosophical. That justifies approaching the document with the hypothesis that it indeed comprises a cogent statement of a philosophical system: harmonious in method, program, and – so I must claim as well – proposition. For, it is now clear, we deal with a rhetoric peculiarly suited to *Listenwissenschaft*, the comparison and contrast of like and unlike, and a logic of cogent discourse that is particularly suitable for philosophical thought of precisely the kind that (I maintain) the Mishnah's framers have done in producing their writing. To what purpose? To make what philosophical point? In Parts Two and beyond I shall answer that question within the limits of the document.

2

Medium and Message in the Pentateuch and the Mishnah: Rhetoric and Logic as Modes of Discourse

The Mishnah's authorship claims to present a system, not a tradition. That explains why, if in detail most of the sixty-one tractates of the Mishnah are readily distinguished from Scripture, in general they conduct discourse in such a way that any relationship at all with a prior writing is, if not denied, then at least subordinated. The bridge from proposition, that is, *what* people think, to process, *how* they think, is built of modes of discourse. For the character of mishnaic discourse, more then the content thereof, demonstrates the intent of the authorship to speak philosophically about propositions that yielded philosophy.

The authorship has not appealed to Scripture for its modes of holding distinct thoughts together in a coherent statement; it does not frame its ideas as a commentary for example, let alone as an amplification of the sense and application of scriptural law. And still more blatant, the difference between the Hebrew of Scripture and the Hebrew of the Mishnah testifies to utter indifference concerning continuity with Scripture. Shifting language from scriptural and therefore archaic Hebrew, such as we find in the Essene writings of the Dead Sea, to an essentially new syntax and fresh morphology, such as we find in the Mishnah, requires us to focus attention upon the character of discourse, not only its non-scriptural or ascriptural contents. To state matters simply, in Scripture, a narrative form joins with a teleological logic to present cogent discourse, while in the Mishnah, a philosophical form joins with propositional logic, specifically, syllogistic and taxonomic logic, to make possible cogent discourse. These are profoundly different modes of discourse indeed, each serving its own well-defined purpose in a well-crafted piece of writing or canon of such writings. Now to spell out what I mean.

First things first: precisely what do I mean by "discourse"? The word refers to the way in which people so formulate statements that the connections within the sequences of the smallest whole units of thought ("sentences") and propositions that comprise their thought are intelligible. Intelligibility by definition refers to cogency, hence the recurrent stress on the public dimension of philosophy. To describe the modes of discourse that attest to modes of thought at the deep structure of mind and that validate my claim that philosophical thought operates, we ask how people place thought on display. And what is required is not only the conclusions they have reached but also their sense of language, the manner in which they wish to announce and argue in favor of those conclusions; the *way* in which they make their statement of their position.

The formal and extrinsic traits of the writing, the Mishnah, appeal to considerations characteristic of system-builders and are not serviceable to the purposes of tradents, that is, persons who formulate and hand on what they claim forms a tradition beginning somewhere prior to themselves and moving forward to some point long past their own position in the chain. These traits for system-builders involve an orderly representation of a topic wholly within the requirements of the intrinsic and indicative traits of that topic. The mark of a system under construction will be the clear logic deriving from the inner structure of a theme or a problem, an order that tells us this must come before that, and a logic that explains why this coheres with that to yield the other thing. Syllogistic reasoning, creating new and secure knowledge out of a corpus of available facts, attests to system-builders. For they have no appeal but to the traits of things, admitting no privileged propositions, calling upon no facts a priori, or, in concrete terms, making room for no received tradition. What we have then to look for is the mark of the new and discovered, rather than the stigmata of the old and received.

Let us begin with the matter of rhetoric, then proceed to logic and finally to topic. In nearly the whole Mishnah (as in all the other documents within the canon of the same Judaism) highly formalized modes of composition convey ideas. Fixed literary structures (that is, rhetoric) dictate to the authorships of nearly all documents the repertoire of choices available for saying whatever it is that they wish to say. What this means is that individual preferences, personal modes of forming sentences for instance, rarely come into play. Nothing is allowed to remain private and idiosyncratic; speech is public and conventional not only in intent but also in form. Thoughts are set forth in a few well-defined ways, and not in the myriad diverse ways in which, in a less formalized literature, people say their piece. That fact vastly facilitates the comparison of documents, since the range of rhetorical choices is limited to the forms and literary structures paramount in the documents subject to description and analytical comparison, and that range is remarkably circumscribed. Not only so, but the work of comparison is made still more reliable by the very extrinsic character of forms and structures; identifying them is not a matter of taste and judgment.

Once we have defined a form or rhetorical pattern or structure, we know whether it is present by appeal to some few facts that are readily accessible to the naked eye. Consequently, there can be irrefutable proof that one set of forms or literary structures, and not another, predominates in a given document, and that proof can even take the form of the statistics which describe the total number of units of thought subject to description and the proportion of those units of thought that fall into the several defined categories of form or structure, as against the proportion of those that do not. Defining these rhetorical conventions therefore sets forth the first step in describing the documents, one by one, and then comparing them to one another. For the forms or literary structures paramount in one differ from those found useful in another, and hence the work of comparison and contrast commences in the simplest and most extrinsic matter. Only when we establish the distinctive traits of documents by appeal to such external matters, in which matters of taste and judgment do not figure, do we move on to substantive differences of topic and even proposition, in which they do – if we let them.

Let me proceed to some simple definitions, beginning with language for rhetorical analysis. A *form* or *literary structure* comprises a set of rules that dictate those recurrent conventions of expression, organization, or proportion, the grammar and syntax of thought and expression, that occur invariably in the ordinary patterning of language and also are *extrinsic* to the message of the author. The conventions at hand bear none of the particular burden of the author's message, so they are not idiosyncratic but systemic and public. A form or literary structure or language pattern of syntax and grammar imposes upon the individual writer a limited set of choices about how he will convey whatever message he has in mind. Or the formal convention will limit an editor or redactor to an equally circumscribed set of alternatives about how to arrange received materials. These conventions then form a substrate of the literary culture that preserves and expresses the worldview and way of life of the system at hand.

When we can define the form or literary structures, we also can ask about the program and policy of thought – recurrent modes of analysis and exercises of conflict and resolution – that dictate the content of the commentary. For how I think and what the syntax of my language and thought permits me to say dictates what I shall think and why I shall think it: this, not that. How are we to recognize the presence of such structures? On the basis of forms that merely appear to be patterned or extrinsic to particular meaning and so entirely formal, we cannot allege that we have in hand a fixed form or literary structure. Such a judgment would prove subjective. Nor shall we benefit from bringing to the text at hand recurrent syntactic or grammatical patterns shown in *other* texts, even of the same canon of literature, to define conventions for communicating ideas. Quite to the contrary, we find guidance in a simple principle: *A text has to define its own structures for us.* But well-crafted texts – and all texts that are copied and recopied endure because they are solidly put together to serve well-considered purposes – always define their forms through a readily accessible protocol and convention of speech.

Patterning of language is readily discerned, for authors do so simply by repeatedly resorting to a severely circumscribed set of literary conventions and to no others. These patterns, we shall soon see, not only dictate formal syntax and principles of composition but also define the deep structure of logical analysis and the modes of proof for particular propositions of argument. On the basis of inductive evidence alone, therefore, a document will testify that its authors adhere to a fixed canon of literary forms. That canon of forms shows that forms guide the authors to the propositions for, or against, which they choose to argue: the program of the book, not only its plan. If demonstrably present, these forms present an author or editor with a few choices on how ideas are to be organized and expressed in intelligible – again, therefore, public – compositions. So internal evidence and that alone testifies to the form or literary structures of a given text. And when we can identify no limited set of forms or structures but only a mass of fixed forms, randomly employed, we further ask whether the authorship of that document also proposes to argue for or against a limited and identifiable set of propositions.

In form analysis or the study of rhetoric of the Mishnah, the adjective "recurrent" constitutes a redundancy when joined to the noun "structure" or "pattern." For we cannot know that we have a structure if the text under analysis does not repeatedly resort to the presentation of its message through a disciplined structure entirely external to its message on any given point. A pattern used episodically defines nothing about a writing as a whole. And, it follows self-evidently, we do know that we have a structure when the text in hand repeatedly follows recurrent conventions of expression, organization, or proportion *extrinsic* to the message of the author. The form or literary structures or patterns find definition in entirely formal and objective facts: the placement of the key-verse subject to discussion in the composition at hand, the origin of that verse. No subjective or impressionistic judgment intervenes. That is why anyone may replicate the results of form analysis carried on inductively in any rabbinic writing.[1]

Second in order of analysis, as we shall see presently, is the logic of a document. I use the simple word, logic, to stand for the principle of intelligibility and cogency of thought and the expression of thought in public discourse. Logic is what joins one sentence to the next and forms the whole into paragraphs of meaning, intelligible propositions, each with its place and sense in a still larger, accessible system. Because of logic one mind connects to another, public discourse becomes possible, debate on issues of general intelligibility takes place, and an *anthology* of statements about a single subject becomes a *composition* of theorems about that subject. What people think – exegesis in accord with a fixed hermeneutic of the system – knows no limit. How they think makes all the difference. Now to the issue at hand: language and how it is structured.

The Mishnah's language is notional and episodic; it invariably focuses upon specific cases and details of those cases. But it is so framed as to repeat certain rigid patterns of syntax. This rather special language is filled with words for neutral things of humble existence. But because of the peculiar and particular way in which it is formed and formalized, this same language not only adheres to an aesthetic theory but expresses a deeply embedded ontology and methodology of the sacred, specifically of the sacred within the secular, and of the capacity for regulation, therefore for sanctification, within the ordinary. Since that is the principal focus of interest in the inductive exercise to follow, we shall first treat the document's rhetoric and logic. These traits predominate throughout. Only when we reach our sample tractate shall we address the more difficult and special

---

[1]Replicate, but also improve upon those results. All of my form-analytical work has been carried on with attention only to the most gross and crude traits of language-patterning. Refinement will show many more patterns and a much more subtle and intricate sense for implicit structure – poetic structure, I should claim – than I have found it necessary to display for the purpose of my sustained and encompassing demonstration of the traits of the literature as a whole. Now that this work is done, a second generation of form analysis can render it obsolete.

problem of identifying a program of principles that I allege underlies the topical repertoire of a given tractate.

The Mishnah's authorship everywhere (in sixty-three of the sixty-four tractates, tractate Avot being the exception) organizes discourse in a topical way and also expresses its ideas in highly formalized language. Let me summarize the criteria of linguistic formalization and editorial organization of the Mishnah, criteria that apply throughout. There are two criteria that account for the organization of the entire document and all but one of its tractates: subject matter and form. The one is topical, the other formal.

The first of the two criteria derives from the nature of the principal divisions themselves: subject matter or theme. What it means to organize a document by topics is self-evident: we talk about this subject here, then that subject there. Within a given subject, we identify the subtopic that comes prior to some other when we know what I must know first to understand the subject, and what I may know only later on in the same sequence of exposition. So the topical organization is familiar to us, since most of the information we receive comes to us within that simple manner of setting things out.

Topical organization – already a familiar conception, since Meilah has shown us how the topic governs not only the materials to enter a tractate but also the way in which those materials will be set forth – necessarily results from a choice. And the possibility of making a choice is readily demonstrated: people could have done things in diverse ways, but they chose only one way for their work. Evidence of what they did decide to do is the document itself; evidence of what they could have done derives from documents to which we know they had access, Scripture presenting the ineluctable instance. We have already taken note, if briefly, that there were (and are) other ways of organizing a piece of writing besides the abstract one of a subject and its inner requirements of order, e.g., what, in that subject, comes first, and what must I know then. One can organize by number sequences, e.g., there are five this's and five that's; by names of authorities, e.g., Rabbi X rules on the following five discrete subjects; by language patterns, e.g., There is no difference between this and that except for the other thing, and the like. All of these modes of organizing thought do occur in the Mishnah.

But, as our case has shown us, there is only one paramount principle of cogent order, and that is defined by the requirements of the exposition of a topic and its indicative traits. It is along thematic lines that the redactors organized vast corpora of materials into principal divisions, tractates. These fundamental themes themselves were subdivided into smaller conceptual units. The principal divisions treat their themes in units indicated by the sequential unfolding of their inner logical structure.

By a "paragraph" (which is a metaphor drawn from our own circumstance) I mean a completed exposition of thought, the setting forth of a complete proposition, now without regard to the larger function, e.g., in a sustained discourse of argument or proposition, served by that thought. Two or more lapidary statements, e.g., allegations as to fact, will make up such a sustained cognitive unit. And collections of such units form chapters, or what I call "intermediate units." Intermediate divisions of these same principal divisions (we might call them chapters of tractates or books) are to be discerned on the basis of internal evidence, through the confluence of theme and form. That is to say, a given intermediate division of a principal one (a chapter of a tractate) will be marked by a particular, recurrent, formal pattern in accord with which sentences are constructed, and also by a particular and distinct theme to which these sentences are addressed. When a new theme commences, a fresh formal pattern will be used.

And this now brings us back to the point with which we commenced, which is the matter of the formalization of syntax or forms. Within the intermediate divisions, we are able to recognize the components, or smallest whole units of thought (hereinafter, cognitive units, defined presently), because there will be a recurrent pattern of sentence structure repeated time and again within the unit and a shifting at the commencement of the next theme. Each point at which the recurrent pattern commences marks the beginning of a new cognitive unit. In general, an intermediate division will contain a carefully enumerated sequence of exempla of cognitive units in the established formal pattern, commonly in groups of three or five or multiples of three or five (pairs for the first division). A single rhetorical pattern will govern the whole set of topical instances of a logical proposition. When the logical-topical program changes, the rhetorical pattern will change too. So the mnemonics of the Mishnah and the foundations of its discourse alike rest on the confluence of (1) deep logic, (2) articulated topic, and (3) manifest rhetoric.

Before proceeding, let me give a concrete case of how the Mishnah is so formulated as to facilitate memorization.

3:11

    A.   Honeycombs: from what point are they susceptible to uncleanness in the status of liquid?

    B.   The House of Shammai say, "When one smokes out [the bees from the combs, so that one can potentially get at the honey]."

    C.   The House of Hillel say, "When one will actually have broken up [the honeycombs to remove the honey]."

M[ishnah-tractate] UQS[in]

The authors begin with an announcement of the topic at hand,
honeycombs, and then ask our question, A. We have a single sentence by
way of an answer:

> *Honeycombs: from what point are they susceptible to uncleanness in*
> *the status of liquid? When ["it is from the point at which"] one smokes*
> *out [the bees from the combs, so that one can get at the honey].*

or:

> *Honeycombs: from what point are they susceptible to uncleanness in*
> *the status of liquid? "When one will actually have broken up [the*
> *honeycombs to remove the honey]."*

We see, therefore, a question followed by a selection of answers, and
each answer can stand on its own to respond to the question. Not only so,
but the simple analysis involving identifying successive sentences
shows us how the sentences are broken up and brought together into a
single coherent statement. This is done by creating a dispute out of
several autonomous statements. We assign a statement to an authority,
the Houses of Shammai and Hillel. Then we make all the statements
bearing attributions into a sequence of responses to a simple problem,
thus a dispute. The formulation of the passage is very tight, a kind of
poetry. For the Hebrew shows closer balance than does the English,
since, at M. Uqs. 3:11, the statements of the two Houses are made up of
precisely the same number of syllables. So the match is more precise
than we would have expected.

We need hardly notice that it is very easy to memorize such highly
patterned language. In point of fact, most of the Mishnah is written not
in narrative prose, flowing declarative sentences for instance, but in
these brief thought units with a question (normally implicit) and an
answer, set forth in a disciplined way. There will be a set of thought
units following a single syntactic and grammatical pattern. Put
together, they will set forth three or five cases, and if you reflect on
the examples, you can readily recover the principle that explains all
three or five rulings. Accordingly, we deal with a piece of writing quite
different from simple narrative, in that the author wants us to learn
the point by putting together things that are given to us to draw a
conclusion that is not spelled out for us – a very warm compliment to us
as readers.

What is at stake in the analysis of rhetoric (and logic) is the
representation of the Mishnah as an autonomous and free-standing
statement of a system. And before I can undertake to describe the
philosophy that that systemic document is meant to set forth, I have to

complete the task of demonstrating that the writing has made its choices, and that these choices clearly and unmistakably reject another protocol all together, that of Scripture (in the Pentateuch in particular).   The standard representation of the Mishnah as a secondary and derivative statement of Scripture, an exegetical document of amplification and clarification, precludes the reading of the document as a representation of a philosophical system, so I have emphasized several times now.   Therefore the comparison of the Mishnah's paramount traits with those of Scripture is required.   When we see the differences, we also perceive what is at stake.

As is characteristic of any well-crafted system, the whole of the pentateuchal writings, as they were finally arranged and put together, is so aimed at making a single cogent statement.   And when we can identify that statement we find our way toward the inner structures that impart to that statement proportion, composition, logical relationship and – it follows – cogency.   That yields the possibility of comparing cogency to cogency, pentateuchal rationality of form and structure with mishnaic rationality of form and structure.

Thus far, in referring to the imputed relationship of the Mishnah to Scripture, I have accepted the premise of the question, that such a relationship must be examined.   But why a relationship with the Pentateuch in particular?   It is not merely because people say that the Mishnah complements the Pentateuch and serves merely as an exegesis and amplification of it, though that is the commonplace position.   It is because of all the components of Scripture, only the Pentateuch is to be compared with the Mishnah.   The basis for comparison explains why. The Mishnah constitutes a systemic statement, and, essentially, a closed system at that, nearly all the information required for making sense of the whole being contained in one or another place within the parts.   And within Scripture the same is so only of the Pentateuch. Alone in the Pentateuch do we find an encompassing and cogent statement composed of an account of a way of life, a worldview, and an "Israel" that in its everyday life realizes the one and accounts for its society and, therefore, its history through the other.   It is the simple fact that all other scriptural writings stand in relationship to that system *au fond*.   They either are arranged in succession to, therefore in relationship with, that system, for example, the historical books, Joshua, Judges, Samuel, and Kings.   Or they make no pretense at exhibiting a systemic character at all.   In all other scriptural books we look in vain, for example, for a picture of how people are to live, of who they are as a social entity, of the way the world is composed and to be explained.   The compilers of Jeremiah, the authors of Psalms, the collectors of Proverbs – these estimable circles in no way provide the prescription for an entire social world.

The history of the Pentateuch *as a systemic statement* begins with the ultimate formation into a cogent composite of diverse writings. Where those materials came from, for whom they spoke to begin with, what they meant prior to their restatement in the context and system they now comprise, define questions the answers to which have no bearing whatsoever upon the systemic analysis of those writings. For the system begins whole, and what system-builders do with received materials is whatever they wish to do with them. As I have already insisted, they do not recognize themselves as bound by prior and original authors' intent, and neither are we so bound in interpreting the outcome of the work of composition and (re)statement. Like the Mishnah, the pentateuchal mosaic read whole forms the model of a closed system, describing as it does the worldview, way of life, social entity, past, present, and future, from beginning to end, all together and in what is transparently a complete way. Details of rules, of course, are tacitly taken for granted; the structure as a whole is encompassing. That is why I claim we deal with a complete and therefore closed system. The pentateuchal mosaic forms a system with an origin (Eden, Sinai) but without a secular history (this king, that king), addressed to a present that has only a future but no pertinent past. But even when read in that way, does the pentateuchal mosaic conform to the definition of a system just now given? And how shall we know? In the two requisite dimensions of such a definition, worldview and way of life, it does, and in the other indicative traits of a system, social focus and intent, it does as well.

For the pentateuchal mosaic, composite though it is, has been so formed as to frame a question and answer that question, forming remarkably disparate materials into a statement of coherence and order. A mark of a closed system is that everything is in the right place, so that, were we to put something in a position other than where it now stands, it would be incomprehensible and the system would fall out of kilter. The question that is answered in the pentateuchal system encompasses a variety of issues, but it always is one question: what, and who, is Israel in relationship to the land? In the aftermath of 586, the "exile," followed by ca. 530, the "return to Zion," that question certainly demanded attention among those few whose families had both gone into exile and returned to Zion, and the pentateuchal mosaic was compiled by the priests among them in particular as an account of the temple, cult, and priesthood in the center and heart of the way of life, worldview, and social entity of the particular "Israel" the priests proposed to make up.

That explains why the question from the beginning in Genesis to the conclusion at the eve of entry into the land in Deuteronomy is, what are the conditions for the formation of the union of Israel with the enchanted land it is to occupy? It also accounts for the ineluctable and persuasive character of the answer, once again encompassing a variety of details: the pentateuchal "Israel," defined like the priesthood by genealogy, formed the family become holy people, and that genealogical "Israel" possesses the land by reason of the covenant of its father-founders, Abraham, Isaac, and Jacob. That covenant is given detail and substance with the forming of the people at Sinai. Israel the people possesses the land not as a given but as a gift, subject to stipulations.

The fundamental systemic statement repetitiously and in one detail after another answers the question of why Israel has lost the land of Israel and what it must do to hold on to it once again. Accordingly, in a single statement we may set forth the systemic message: God made the land and gave it to Israel on condition that Israel do what God demands. That is the answer. It also leads us to define the ineluctable question, that demands this answer, the question that presses and urgently insists upon an answer. In the circumstance, after the destruction of the Temple of Jerusalem in 586 B.C., of the formation of the pentateuchal composition and system, the question is equally accessible. It is, why has Israel lost the land, and what does Israel have to do now to hold on to it again?

These remarks draw us away from the main issue of this chapter, which concerns the comparison of rhetoric. But when we take note of how the framers presented their work, we see the abyss that separates the rhetoric of the Mishnah from that of Scripture. The comparison shows us that, to make their points, the system-builders of the Pentateuch have appealed to narrative (just as, in the following chapter, we shall find striking their appeal to the logic of cogent discourse deriving from teleology, not from syllogism). When the authorship(s) of the Pentateuch, as their work has finally been assembled, wish to prove a point, it is by telling a story. The Pentateuch uses narrative even when it does not have to, e.g., prefacing laws with occasions on which laws are set forth. The Mishnah does not use narrative even when it would handsomely serve its strategy of exposition, for instance, in its account of the impact of the destruction of the Temple on the liturgy of the synagogue in Mishnah-tractate Rosh Hashshanah, or in its picture of the observance of the Sabbatical Year in Mishnah-tractate Shebiit, to give two blatant instances. And where Mishnah's authorship does use narrative, as in its pictures of Temple rites (e.g., Mishnah-tractate Negaim, Chapter Fourteen, Mishnah-tractate Parah, Chapter Three), the narrative is never specific and concrete, always general and intended to illustrate abstract principles of right procedure.

When, through a large portion of the whole, the Pentateuch devotes time and attention to the matter of the cult, it tells the story to make the point. Then stories will concern the centrality of sacrifice, the founding of the priesthood and its rules, and the importance of the Temple in Jerusalem. This is done, for instance, through those many stories of Genesis that are aimed at explaining the origin, in the lives and deeds of the patriarchs, of the locations of various cultic centers prior to the centralization of the cult in Jerusalem, the beginnings of the priesthood, the care and feeding of priests, the beginnings and rules of the sacrificial system, the contention between priestly castes, e.g., Levites and priests, and diverse other matters. Much of Exodus is devoted to the description, within the context of an overarching narrative, of the tabernacle in the wilderness as prototype of the Temple. The description is given an artificial, narrative form by identifying the makers and what they did, or are to do, on some one day. It is through these narratives that the system links the whole of the social order to the cult, and that is what imparts to the system its distinctive structure and conveys its urgent messages. It is solely through the forms of narrative and the logic of cogent discourse provided by narrative that the pentateuchal authorships set forth their picture of the system's Israel. That is how they represented the system's "kingdom of priests" ruled by priests, its "holy people" living out the holiness imparted by obedience to the covenant, as a matter of fact laid claim to the authority of God's revelation to Moses at Sinai.

Now, as a matter of fact, nothing is presented as tradition formed out of a long chain of incremental and sedimentary formation. It was all together, all at once, one time, with no past other than the past made up for the system, not process, not justified by ancient custom. But the medium of expressing the system is what is at stake here, and that medium is, as I have pointed out, one or another genre of narrative.

In Chapter One we have noted how the pentateuchal system clearly rejects the philosophical and chooses the teleological approach to finding out how one thing links up with some other and to drawing conclusions from that connection. Here it suffices to note that discourse is sustained through accounts of what are deemed to be events, and, in consequence, the principal mode of sustained discourse is the telling of stories. The worldview of the system emerges in particular through these stories. When the system-builders wish to account for the identification of the social entity, "Israel," they tell the story of the founders, the patriarchs and matriarchs, and what happened to them. "Israel" then comes into being through the story of how the family became the people. The laws of the system, its way of life, are set forth within a narrative setting, e.g., revelation at Sinai, in Exodus, the circumstance and the speaker and the authority, in Leviticus and Numbers. Not only so, but even where the laws are laid out essentially independent of narrative, as in Deuteronomy, the laws as a whole are laid out in a tight relationship to a story, so that the fictive setting provides what the system deems absolutely essential. In these and other instances we discern the system's general conception that connection derives from sequence, first this, then that, hence that is because of this. Then the drawing of conclusions derives from connections discerned between this and that: one event, then another event, and the cause that links the latter to the former and explains the order of things. We may now say very simply that as to rhetoric, there is no meaningful connection between the choices made by the system-builders of the Pentateuch and those that served the purposes of the system-builders of the Mishnah. When we find philosophical modes of speech in the Mishnah, they therefore represent preferences, not merely habits. There were other ways of speaking, other media for registering points. But our authorship found the philosophical ones, with their abstraction and their susceptibility to generalization, serviceable. These cursory remarks suffice to characterize the writing before us as the result of making choices and to justify my description of those choices as independent of Scripture's mode of discourse. We now are ready to address the other indicative trait of the mind that stands behind a system and its written expression: the philosophical medium and message of the document as conveyed by its logic and its sustained debate about the premises of being, which I call its medium (of thought).

If the strict conventions of forms and literary structures make their mark on the surface of documents, the inquiry into its logic of cogent discourse, a term explained immediately, carries us to the depths of the structures of thought of those same documents. In the case of the Mishnah's philosophers, if we wish to know how they thought about things, we begin with how they represented the conclusions that they drew. That representation, in the form of cogent paragraphs made up of coherent sentences, leads us into the thought processes that produced the conclusions of our writing. For while rhetoric dictates the material arrangement of words, logic governs the possibilities of thought. It defines how thought, arranged or set forth in one way, makes sense, and, arranged and set forth in another way, yields nonsense.

What makes the inquiry interesting is that, in any sustained and systematic piece of writing, we can address the single telling question of whether the rhetoric and the logic fit together in carrying out, or even giving expression to, the document's fundamental purpose and message. In a well-crafted system, expressed in a fine piece of writing, one result will emerge; whether we explore the extrinsic traits of formal expression or the most profound layers of intelligible discourse and coherent thought that hold sentences together and form of them all propositions or presentations that can be understood, we should produce a single result. It is that the well-crafted document's authorship does make choices in such a way as to work out a rationality of its own. Choosing modes of cogent discourse and coherent thought involves limiting thought within a repertoire that is already exceedingly limited. Options in rhetoric have already indicated how, within a quite diverse literary-rhetorical heritage, people selected some few ways of saying a great many things. And that is not an imposed position. With regard to both rhetoric and logic we are required to compare fixed and external traits. In all that follows there is – and can be – no appeal to subjective taste and individual judgment.

It is philosophy that accomplishes the miracle of making the whole more – or less – than the sum of the parts, that is, in the simple language I have used up to now, showing the connections between fact 1 and fact 2, so as to yield proposition A. We begin with the irrefutable fact; our issue is not how facts gain their facticity, rather, how, from givens, people construct propositions or make statements that are deemed sense and nonsense or gibberish. So the problem is to explain the connections between and among facts, so accounting for the conclusions people draw, on the one side, or the acceptable associations people tolerate, on the other, in the exchange of language and thought. Propositional logic also may be syllogistic, e.g., a variant on a famous syllogistic argument:

1. All Greeks are philosophers.
2. Demosthenes is a Greek.
3. Therefore Demosthenes is a philosopher.

At issue is not mere facticity, rather, broadly speaking, the *connections* between facts.

The problem subject to analysis here is how one thing follows from something else, or how one thing generates something else, thus, as I said, connection. Connection is accomplished by appeal to the intrinsic or inherent traits of what is connected. And all things depend upon relationship. How relationship is established between unrelated things defines the logic at hand, and it is through the traits of the unrelated things: comparison and contrast. In that context, then, the sentences 1, 2, and 3, standing entirely by themselves convey not a proposition but merely statements of a fact, which may or may not be true, and which may or may not bear sense and meaning beyond themselves. Sentence 1 and sentence 2 by themselves state facts but announce no proposition. But the logic of syllogistic discourse joins the two into No. 3, which indeed does constitute a proposition and also shows the linkage between sentence 1 and sentence 2. But there are more ways for setting forth propositions, making points, and thus for undertaking intelligible discourse, besides the philosophical and syllogistic one with which we are familiar in the West. We know a variety of other modes of philosophical-propositional discourse, that is to say, presenting, testing, and demonstrating a proposition through appeal to fact and argument.

Earlier I characterized the paramount logic of intelligible discourse as well as the complementary one. Now my task is to show that there were other logics, available but not utilized, and to demonstrate that these other logics cannot have served the philosophical program of our authorship. I present not only positive evidence in favor of my hypothesis concerning the character of the document, but also negative evidence against the contrary hypothesis. For that purpose we turn to not one but two available logics, the teleological, on the one side, the fixed associative, on the other. Neither served, though not for the same reason as excluded the other. Let us deal first with the teleological logic of cogent and intelligent discourse, because this logic does establish propositions; but the propositions do not derive from the intrinsic traits of things but rather their place in some larger plan, their purpose, their teleology. And that appeal is contrary to the one that, as we have seen, operates in the Mishnah.

Teleological logic is familiar to us. We recognize that a proposition emerges not only through philosophical argument and analysis, e.g., spelling out in so many words a general and encompassing proposition, and further constructing in proof of that explicit generalization a syllogism and demonstration. We may state and demonstrate a proposition in a logic that resorts to teleology expressed through narrative (itself subject to a taxonomy of its own) both to establish and to explain connections between naked facts. Within the narrative the teleology serves to connect one sentence, fact, or thought, to another. A proposition (whether or not it is stated explicitly) may be set forth and demonstrated by showing through the telling of a tale (of a variety of kinds, e.g., historical, fictional, parabolic, and the like) that a sequence of events, real or imagined, shows the ineluctable truth of a given proposition.

Before proceeding, let me give a concrete instance of teleological logic as portrayed in the pentateuchal statement. Here we see that telological logic, dictating the connections we make and the conclusions we draw, appeals to goal or purpose, for example, as displayed in history. What links together the sentences that follow is the goal stated at the outset. In achieving this goal, these are the things that one must do. But the things do not relate at all within their inherent or intrinsic traits. The sentences are discrete, not topically or logically related to one another. And each sentence finds its place in context for the same reason. It is another way to achieve that purpose set forth at the head. Lev. 19:1-18 (given in the Revised Standard Version) provides our instance of teleological connection among otherwise unrelated facts/sentences:

> And the Lord said to Moses, "Say to all the congregation of the people of Israel, You shall be holy, for I the Lord your God am holy.
>
> "Every one of you shall revere his mother and his father and you shall keep my Sabbaths, I am the Lord your God.
>
> "Do not turn to idols or make for yourselves molten gods; I am the Lord your God.
>
> "When you offer a sacrifice of peace-offerings to the Lord, you shall offer it so that you may be accepted. It shall be eaten the same day you offer it or on the morrow, and anything left over until the third day shall be burned with fire. If it is eaten at all on the third day, it is an abomination, it will not be accepted, and every one who eats it shall bear his iniquity, because he has profaned a holy thing of the Lord; and that person shall be cut off from his people.
>
> "When you reap the harvest of your land, you shall not reap your field to its very border, neither shall you gather the gleanings after your harvest. And you shall not strip your vineyard bare, neither shall you gather the fallen grapes of your vineyard; you shall leave them for the poor and for the sojourner. I am the Lord your God.
>
> "You shall not steal, nor deal falsely, nor lie to one another. And you shall not swear by my name falsely and so profane the name of your God; I am the Lord. You shall not oppress your neighbor or rob him. The wages of a hired servant shall not remain with you all night until the morning. You shall not curse the deaf or put a stumbling block before the blind, but you shall fear your God; I am the Lord.
>
> "You shall do no injustice in judgment; you shall not be partial to the poor or defer to the great, but in righteousness shall you judge your neighbor. You shall not go up and down as a slanderer among your people, and you shall not stand forth against the life of your neighbor; I am the Lord.
>
> "You shall not hate your brother in your heart, but you shall reason with your neighbor, lest you bear sin because of him. You shall not take vengeance or bear any grudge against the sons of your own people, but you shall love your neighbor as yourself; I am the Lord."

Except for the opening and closing lines of the pericope, the linkage of sentence to sentence (treating the paragraphs as sentences) is hardly self-evident.   These are all things that, unrelated to one another, relate to the goal of sanctification.   This mixture of rules we should regard as cultic as to sacrifice, moral as to support of the poor, ethical as to right-dealing, and above all religious as to "being holy for I the Lord your God am holy" – the rules all together portray a complete and whole society: its worldview, holiness in the likeness of God, its way of life, an everyday life of sanctification through the making of distinctions, its Israel: Israel.   The definition of who is Israel lay at the foundation of the system, which was shaped to answer that urgent question of social explanation.   That is what holds the whole together, and, we see, the principle of cogent discourse appeals to teleology expressed as a kind of narrative.

And this brings us back to the argument of this chapter.   That people made choices as to the appropriate logic for their discourse emerges in the contrast between the Mishnah's and the Pentateuch's choices in this matter.   The composite produced by the pentateuchal authorship provides an account of how things were in order to explain how things are and set forth how they should be, with the tabernacle in the wilderness the model for (and modeled after) the temple in the Jerusalem a building.   The Mishnah speaks in a continuing present tense, saying only how things are, indifferent to the *were* and the *will be.* The Pentateuch focuses upon self-conscious "Israel," saying who they were and what they must become to overcome how they now are.   The Mishnah understands by "Israel" as much the individual as the nation and identifies as its principal actors, the heroes of its narrative, not the family become a nation, but the priest and the householder, the woman and the slave, the adult and the child, and other castes and categories of person within an inward-looking, established, fully landed community.   Given the Mishnah's authorship's interest in classifications and categories, therefore in systematic hierarchization of an orderly world, one can hardly find odd that (re)definition of the subject matter and problematic of the systemic social entity.

While, therefore, the Pentateuch appeals to the logic of teleology to draw together and make sense of facts, so making connections by appeal to the end and drawing conclusions concerning the purpose of things, the Mishnah's authorship knows only the philosophical logic of syllogism, the rule-making logic of lists.   The pentateuchal logic reached concrete expression in narrative, which served to point to the direction and goal of matters, hence, in the nature of things, of history. Accordingly, those authors, when putting together diverse materials,

so shaped everything as to form of it all as continuous a narrative as
they could construct, and through that "history" that they made up,
they delivered their message and also portrayed that message as
cogent and compelling.

What distinguishes the two logics – the Mishnah's philosophical-
syllogistic, the Pentateuch's teleological-narrative – also explains the
contrasting selection of systemically important facts characteristic of
each writing. For once the system-builders know the facts they wish to
address, they also will discern connections between those facts and no
others. The logic of connection depends upon the logic of drawing
conclusions from connection. And conclusions derive from a prior
recognition of questions we wish to answer. For one example deriving
from Scripture, hence to be compared and contrasted with our example
from the Mishnah, I may posit, by way of a mental experiment, a
simple case: the connection between the destruction of the Temple, the
exile to Babylonia, and the return to Zion, a connection implicit in the
pentateuchal narrative seen whole. That connection is self-evident in
the Pentateuch.

But it will not have struck as self-evident, demanding a particular
choice of systemically active facts and rejection of systemically inert
ones, a family that remained in Babylonia, for that family did not
return to Zion. To the thought that such a family may be devoted to
their social circumstances, the return to Zion will have proved not
inevitable, not ineluctable, and, indeed, not categorically formative,
for, as the facts of the social existence demonstrated, that fact changed
nothing and affected nothing.[2] If the logic in play is one that
identified *this, then that*, yielding the proposition, *this, joined to
that*, and so generating the conclusion, *that, because of this*, then a
different set of facts will have demanded attention from facts that, to

---

[2]Let me clarify this point briefly. From the perspective of a vast Israelite
population, namely, Jews who had remained in the land, Jews who had never
left Babylonia, Jews living in other parts of the world, such as Egypt, the system
spoke of events that simply had never happened or had not happened in the
way that the pentateuchal mosaic claims. For the systemic conclusions
invoked no self-evidently valid connections, when people had no data out of
their own, or their family's, experience, on the basis of which to make such
connections. Consider the Jews who remained in the land after 586, or those
who remained in Babylonia after Cyrus's decree permitting the return to Zion.
For both groups, for different reasons, there was no alienation, also,
consequently, no reconciliation, and the normative corresponded to the merely
normal: life like any other nation, wherever it happened to locate itself. And
that ignores Jews in Egypt, Mesopotamia, and other parts of the world of the
time who were not in the Land when it was captured and who also were not
taken captive to Babylonia.

such a family, made no difference to begin with. The facts found noteworthy to begin with found consequence in the system that identified *those* facts and not other facts. The pentateuchal system chose facts that narrative conveyed and logic interpreted; the mishnaic system chose other facts, ones that list-making conveyed, and *Listenwissenschaft* interpreted. So we have quite different logics indeed. That fact validates my claim that one logic, and not another one, served philosophy in its form of practical logic and applied reason, but not (as a matter of fact) theology in its form of narrative and within its logic of telelogical cogency.

There is a fourth logic in the canon of the Judaism that commences, after Scripture, with the Mishnah. It is a logic that later on predominated, but that, for the authorship of the Mishnah, was in a concrete sense simply unthinkable. As we have seen, this is the logic of fixed association, by which distinct facts or sentences or thoughts are held together without actually joining into sequential and coherent propositions of any kind. It is the exact opposite of propositional logic, whether philosophical and syllogistic or narrative and teleological.

Megillah 1:5-10

1:5
A. There is no difference between a festival day and the Sabbath day except for preparing food alone [M. Bes. 5:21].
B. There is no difference between the Sabbath and the Day of Atonement except that deliberately violating this one is punishable at the hands of an earthly court, while deliberately violating that one is punishable through extirpation.

1:6
A. There is no difference between one who is prohibited by vow from deriving [general] benefit from his fellow, and one who is prohibited by vow from deriving food from his fellow, except for setting foot in his house and using utensils of his which are not for preparing food [permitted in the former case].
B. There is no difference between vows and freewill-offerings, except that for animals designated in fulfillment of vows one is responsible, while for animals set aside in fulfillment of freewill-offerings one is not responsible [should the animal be lost].

1:7
A. There is no difference between a *Zab* who suffers two appearances of flux and one who suffers three except for the requirement of an offering [for the latter].
B. There is no difference between a *mesora* who is shut up and one who has been certified except for the requirement to mess up the hair and tear the clothing.

C.   There is no difference between [a *mesora*] declared clean having been shut up and one declared clean having been certified [unclean] except for the requirement of shaving and of bringing a bird-offering.

1:8

A.   There is no difference between sacred scrolls and phylacteries and *mezuzot* except that sacred scrolls may be written in any alphabet ["language"], while phylacteries and *mezuzot* are written only in square ["Assyrian"] letters.

B.   Rabban Simeon b. Gamaliel says, "Also: in the case of sacred scrolls: they have been permitted to be written only in Greek."

1:9

A.   There is no difference between a priest who is anointed with anointing oil and one who wears many garments except in the bullock which is offered for unwitting transgression of any of the commandments [required only of the former].

B.   There is no difference between a [high] priest presently in service and [high] priest [who served] in times past except for the bullock which is offered on the Day of Atonement and the tenth of the ephah [cf. M. Hor 3:4].

1:10

A.   There is no difference between a major high place and a minor high place except for Passover-offerings.

No proposition joins any entry to any other. Yet the framer of the passage clearly has presented a deeply cogent formation. And what imparts that cogency is the repeated formula, there is no difference...except, which appeals not to content but to convention – hence, fixed association. A broad variety of such examples of the logic of fixed association within the Mishnah would carry us to examine the excluded Mishnah-tractates, Avot and Eduyyot, which appeal to lists of names to establish cogency. It is then an available logic, one used in two tractates of the sixty-three of which the Mishnah is composed, not used commonly or at all in the other sixty-one.

Finally, can I demonstrate that the readership of the Mishnah identified the logic that predominated and understood its indicative traits, that is, appeal to classification on the basis of intrinsic characteristics of things? Those who inherited the document took a different position on the correct mode of classification – by appeal to the traits of things. I have now to demonstrate that another mode of thought, serving the same purposes and within the same structure of the taxonomic logic of natural philosophy, was available and indeed was selected. Sifra, a sustained address to the book of Leviticus, is a document that stands in close relationship with the Mishnah, which is constantly cited or quoted or alluded to; many chapters of Sifra are intelligible only if we know the counterpart discussions in the Mishnah. That document then provides an appropriate opportunity to test in yet a third way the null hypothesis and the hypothesis alike: that the paramount logic of the Mishnah represents choices some made – *and others rejected*.

Sifra's authorship's critique of the mode of classification chosen by the authorship of the Mishnah now requires attention. Specifically, that authorship recognized the principles of classification by appeal to the traits of things, which we identify as philosophical, and rejected them in favor of another principle. In their view the correct classification of things is dictated only by Scripture, and logic that appeals to intrinsic traits, ignoring the classifications dictated by Scripture, is flawed and unreliable. This other principle of the logical classification of things shows a deep affinity for the logic of fixed association because it appeals to a received and not an intrinsic mode of classification. Specifically, it is *Scripture's* classifications, and not those inherent in things by their very nature, that serves to dictate how we make our lists and so derive our general principles. That fact of logic explains the complementary fact, that Sifra's authorship organizes its propositions through the logic of fixed association, that is, as a commentary. Scripture dictates not only the correct medium of classification but also the correct representation of propositions: coherent only as Scripture imparts coherence.

How does the Sifra's authorship's critique of the logic of cogent discourse of the Mishnah come to expression? The basic critique addressed by Sifra's authorship to the Mishnah's philosophical logic is this: time and again, we can easily demonstrate, things have so many and such diverse and contradictory indicative traits that, comparing one thing to something else, we can always distinguish one species from another. Even though we find something in common, we also can discern some other trait characteristic of one thing but not the other. Consequently, we also can show that the hierarchical logic on which we rely, the argument *a fortiori* or *qol vehomer*, will not serve. For if on the basis of one set of traits which yield a given classification, we place into hierarchical order two or more items on the basis of a different set of traits, we have either a different classification altogether, or, much more commonly, simply a different hierarchy. So the attack on the way in which the Mishnah's authorship has done its work appeals to not merely the limitations of classification solely on the basis of traits of things. The more telling argument addresses what is, to *Listenwissenschaft*, the source of power and compelling proof: hierarchization. That is why, throughout, we must designate the Mishnah's mode of *Listenwissenschaft* a logic of hierarchical classification. Things are not merely like or unlike, therefore following one rule or its opposite. Things also are weightier or less weighty, and that particular point of likeness or difference generates the logical force of *Listenwissenschaft*.

Time and again Sifra's authorship demonstrates that the formation of classifications based on monothetic taxonomy, that is to say, traits that are not only common to both items but that are shared throughout both items subject to comparison and contrast, simply will not serve. For at every point at which someone alleges uniform, that is to say, monothetic likeness, Sifra's authorship will demonstrate difference. Then how to proceed? Appeal to some shared traits as a basis for classification: this is not like that, and that is not like this, but the indicative trait that both exhibit is such and so, that is to say, polythetic taxonomy. The self-evident problem in accepting differences among things and insisting, nonetheless, on their monomorphic character for purposes of comparison and contrast, cannot be set aside: who says? That is, if I can adduce in evidence for a shared classification of things only a few traits among many characteristic of each thing, then what stops me from treating all things alike? Polythetic taxonomy opens the way to an unlimited exercise in finding what diverse things have in common and imposing, for that reason, one rule on everything. Then the very working of *Listenwissenschaft* as a tool of analysis, differentiation, comparison, contrast, and the descriptive determination of rules yields the opposite of what is desired.

Let us consider one sustained example of how Sifra's authorship rejects the principles of the logic of hierarchical classification precisely as these are worked out by the framers of the Mishnah. I emphasize that the critique applies to the way in which a shared logic is worked out by the other authorship. For it is not the principle that like things follow the same rule, unlike things, the opposite rule, that is at stake. Nor is the principle of hierarchical classification embodied in the argument *a fortiori* at issue. What our authorship disputes is that we can classify things on our own by appeal to the traits or indicative characteristics, that is, utterly without reference to Scripture.

The argument is simple. On our own, we cannot classify species into genera. Everything is different from everything else in some way. But Scripture tells us what things are like what other things for what purposes; hence Scripture imposes on things the definitive classifications, that and not traits we discern in the things themselves. When we see the nature of the critique, we shall have a clear picture of what is at stake when we examine, in some detail, precisely how the

Mishnah's logic does its work. That is why at the outset I present a complete composition in which Sifra's authorship tests the modes of classification characteristic of the Mishnah, resting as they do on the traits of things viewed out of the context of Scripture's categories of things.

5. Parashat Vayyiqra Dibura Denedabah

Parashah 3

V:I

1.   A.   "[If his offering is] a burnt-offering [from the herd, he shall offer a male without blemish; he shall offer it at the door of the tent of meeting, that he may be accepted before the Lord; he shall lay his hand upon the head of the burnt-offering, and it shall be accepted for him to make atonement for him]" (Lev. 1:2).

   B.   Why does Scripture refer to a burnt-offering in particular?

   C.   For one might have taken the view that all of the specified grounds for the invalidation of an offering should apply only to the burnt-offering that is brought as a freewill-offering.

   D.   But how should we know that the same grounds for invalidation apply also to a burnt-offering that is brought in fulfillment of an obligation [for instance, the burnt-offering that is brought for a leper who is going through a rite of purification, or the bird brought by a woman who has given birth as part of her purification-rite, Lev. 14, 12, respectively]?

   E.   It is a matter of logic.

   F.   Bringing a burnt-offering as a freewill-offering and bringing a burnt-offering in fulfillment of an obligation [are parallel to one another and fall into the same classification].

   G.   Just as a burnt-offering that is brought as a freewill-offering is subject to all of the specified grounds for invalidation, so to a burnt-offering brought in fulfillment of an obligation, all the same grounds for invalidation should apply.

   H.   No, [that reasoning is not compelling. For the two species of the genus, burnt-offering, are not wholly identical and can be distinguished, on which basis we may also maintain that the grounds for invalidation that pertain to the one do not necessarily apply to the other. Specifically:] if you have taken that position with respect to the burnt-offering brought as a freewill-offering, for which there is no equivalent, will you take the same position with regard to the burnt-offering brought in fulfillment of an obligation, for which there is an equivalent? [For if one is obligated to bring a burnt-offering by reason of obligation and cannot afford a beast, one may bring birds, as at Lev. 14:22, but if one is bringing a freewill-offering, a less expensive form of the offering may not serve.]

   I.   Accordingly, since there is the possibility in the case of the burnt-offering brought in fulfillment of an obligation, in which case there is an acceptable equivalent [to the more expensive beast, through the less expensive birds], all of the specified grounds for invalidation [which apply to the in any case more expensive burnt-offering brought as a freewill-offering] should not apply at all.

J. That is why in the present passage, Scripture refers simply to "burnt-offering," [and without further specification, the meaning is then simple] all the same are the burnt-offering brought in fulfillment of an obligation and a burnt-offering brought as a freewill-offering in that all of the same grounds for invalidation of the beast that pertain to the one pertain also to the other.

2. A. And how do we know that the same rules of invalidation of a blemished beast apply also in the case of a beast that is designated in substitution of a beast sanctified for an offering [in line with Lev. 27:10, so that, if one states that a given, unconsecrated beast is to take the place of a beast that has already been consecrated, the already consecrated beast remains in its holy status, and the beast to which reference is made also becomes consecrated]?

B. The matter of bringing a burnt-offering and the matter of bringing a substituted beast fall into the same classification [since both are offerings that in the present instance will be consumed upon the altar, and, consequently, they fall under the same rule as to invalidating blemishes].

C. Just as the entire protocol of blemishes applies to the one, so in the case of the beast that is designated as a substitute, the same invalidating blemishes pertain.

D. No, if you have invoked that rule in the case of the burnt-offering, in which case no status of sanctification applies should the beast that is designated as a burnt-offering be blemished in some permanent way, will you make the same statement in the case of a beast that is designated as a substitute? For in the case of a substituted beast, the status of sanctification applies even though the beast bears a permanent blemish! [So the two do not fall into the same classification after all, since to begin with one cannot sanctify a permanently blemished beast, which beast can never enter the status of sanctification, but through an act of substitution, a permanently blemished beast can be placed into the status of sanctification.]

E. Since the status of sanctification applies [to a substituted beast] even though the beast bears a permanent blemish, all of the specified grounds for invalidation as a matter of logic should not apply to it.

F. That is why in the present passage, Scripture refers simply to "burnt-offering," [and without further specification, the meaning is then simple:] all the same are the burnt-offering brought in fulfillment of an obligation and a burnt-offering brought as a substitute for an animal designated as holy, in that all of the same grounds for invalidation of the beast that pertain to the one pertain also to the other.

3. A. And how do we know [that the protocol of blemishes that apply to the burnt-offering brought as a freewill-offering apply also to]

animals that are subject to the rule of a sacrifice as a peace-offering?

B. It is a matter of logic. The matter of bringing a burnt-offering and the matter of bringing animals that are subject to the rule of a sacrifice as a peace-offering fall into the same classification [since both are offerings and, consequently, under the same rule as to invalidating blemishes].

C. Just as the entire protocol of blemishes applies to the one, so in the case of animals that are subject to the rule of a sacrifice as a peace-offering, the same invalidating blemishes pertain.

D. And it is furthermore a matter of an argument *a fortiori*, as follows:

E. If a burnt-offering is valid when in the form of a bird, [which is inexpensive], the protocol of invalidating blemishes applies to peace-offerings, which are not valid when brought in the form of a bird, surely the same protocol of invalidating blemishes should also apply!

F. No, if you have applied that rule to a burnt-offering, in which case females are not valid for the offering as male beasts are, will you say the same of peace-offerings? For female beasts as much as male beasts may be brought for sacrifice in the status of the peace-offering. [The two sexes may be distinguished from one another].

G. Since it is the case that female beasts as well as male beasts may be brought for sacrifice in the status of the peace-offering, the protocol of invalidating blemishes should not apply to a beast designated for use as peace-offerings.

H. That is why in the present passage, Scripture refers simply to "burnt-offering," [and without further specification, the meaning is then simple:] all the same are the burnt-offering brought in fulfillment of an obligation and an animal designated under the rule of peace-offerings, in that all of the same grounds for invalidation of the beast that pertain to the one pertain also to the other.

The systematic exercise proves for beasts that serve in three classifications of offerings, burnt-offerings, substitutes, and peace-offerings, that the same rules of invalidation apply throughout. The comparison of the two kinds of burnt-offerings, voluntary and obligatory, shows that they are sufficiently different from one another so that as a matter of logic, what pertains to the one need not apply to the other. Then come the differences between an animal that is consecrated and one that is designated as a substitute for one that is consecrated. Finally we distinguish between the applicable rules of the sacrifice; a burnt-offering yields no meat for the person in behalf of whom the offering is made, while one sacrificed under the rule of peace-offerings does. What is satisfying, therefore, is that we run the changes on three fundamental differences and show that in each case, the differences between like things are greater than the similarities. I cannot imagine a more perfect exercise in the applied and practical logic of comparison and contrast.

The upshot is very simple. The authorship of Sifra concurs in the fundamental principle that right thinking requires discovering the classification of things and determining the rule that governs diverse things. How that authorship differs from the view of the Mishnah's concerns – I emphasize – *the origins of taxa*: how do we know what diverse things form a single classification of things. Taxa originate in Scripture. Accordingly, at stake in the critique of the Mishnah is not the principles of logic necessary for understanding the construction and inner structure of creation. All parties among sages concurred that the inner structure set forth by a logic of classification alone could sustain the system of ordering all things in proper place and under the proper rule. The like belongs with the like and conforms to the rule governing the like, the unlike goes over to the opposite and conforms to the opposite rule. When we make lists of the like, we also know the rule governing all the items on those lists, respectively. We know that and one other thing, namely, the opposite rule, governing all items sufficiently like to belong on those lists, but sufficiently unlike to be placed on other lists. That rigorously philosophical logic of analysis, comparison and contrast, served because it was the only logic that could serve a system that proposed to make the statement concerning order and right array. Let us first show how the logic of proving propositions worked, then review Sifra's authorship's systematic critique of the way in which the Mishnah's framers applied that logic, specifically, proposed to identify classifications.

The argument of Sifra's authorship is that, by themselves, things do not possess traits that permit us finally to classify species into a common genus. There always are traits distinctive to a classification. Accordingly, it is the argument of Sifra's authorship that without the revelation of the Torah we are not able to effect any classification at all. We are left, that is to say, only with species, no genus, only with cases, no rules. That appeal to Scripture forms the counterpart, in analytical logic, to the principle of cogent discourse that rests upon the dictated order of verses of Scripture, that is, the logic of fixed association. The authorship of the Mishnah appeals to philosophical logic of classification and philosophical logic of cogent discourse, and in doing so, we now realize, it made choices others recognized and rejected.

We have come a long way in this effort to demonstrate a simple fact. It is that the logic that imparts cogency to the discourse of the Mishnah represents a choice, and the choice is a philosophical preference as against other possible preferences: theological, over the pentateuchal logic of teleological connection, systemic, over the Sifra's logic of conventional (they would say, revealed) connection. We may now turn to the Mishnah's philosophy because we understand the system's logic and can classify it as philosophical. That justifies treating the document as I shall, as a cogent statement of a philosophical system: method, program, proposition. For, it is now clear, we deal with a logic of cogent discourse that is particularly suitable for philosophical thought of precisely the kind that (I maintain) the Mishnah's framers have done in producing their writing.

The (demonstrably) available repertoire of logics shows us that the Mishnah's authorship has selected a free-standing document, which everywhere appeals for cogency and coherence to the traits of things. Our review of the modes of thought that the authorship did not deem serviceable proved, from another perspective, the Mishnah's autonomous and free-standing, essentially systematic stance. That conclusion now makes possible the inquiry into the philosophical structure and system that, I maintain, the authorship has adumbrated in this writing.

The stakes thus have proved as high here as they were when we asked about the relationship of Mishnah-tractate Meilah to Scripture. If scriptural, then not philosophical, and, if philosophical, then not scriptural: so the rule of thumb instructed. Here, a logic that does not sustain systematic and autonomous discourse, resting on the traits of what is discussed, permits no talk of an abstract and cogent philosophical structure and system. But the logic of the Mishnah turns out to be a philosophical logic of proposition and syllogism, and then we can have philosophy in what is said. What, precisely, is that message? Why do I claim it is philosophical? The next part of the book answers these questions.

Part Two
THE MESSAGE THROUGH THE MEDIUM

3

Revelation and Reason, Scripture and Mishnah

When we formulate the question of the relationship of the Mishnah to Scripture, we adopt the language and categories that the authorship of the Mishnah wanted us to use. For (to personify that authorship in the name of Judah the Patriarch) what the Patriarch accomplished through remarkably adroit imposition of uniform rhetoric and logic upon the discussion of discrete, topical materials was precisely that: to treat everything as one thing. Hence we rightly identify "the Mishnah" as a single work. We see it as uniform because whatever topic it discusses among its sixty-one relevant tractates (I omit reference to Pirqé Abot as outside of the entire rhetorical, logical, and topical program of the document, and to Eduyyot as a mere reprise), the authorship of the Mishnah does what appears to be the same thing. That is to say, that authorship formulates its ideas within a strikingly limited formal repertoire. It appeals for cogency to a narrow range of logical possibilities, generally limited to what we know as *Listenwissenschaft*, that is, the making of lists that in detail register a single general rule (about which I shall have more to say), and, throughout, preserves a remarkable cogency of style.

But what if we introduce analytical variables of our own making? Then the unity and uniformity of the Mishnah prove to conceal considerable diversity. The sixty-one tractates of the Mishnah, each analyzed on its own, turn out to yield as much diversity in structure – e.g., relationship to other writings – as they do in topic. And we must not be deceived by the authorship's genius in its uniform formalization of the whole to assume that the topical differentiation that that same authorship has adopted for its organizing principle effects difference merely at the surface of things. For while the Mishnah's authorship has made things appear as though all that differs, in the vast cogent writing, is subject matter, subject-matter matters. That is to say, differences in topic from one tractate to another (and one division to another) prove very real and contradict uniformity in rhetoric and even in prevailing logic.

And if that is the case, it must follow, the relationships between the document and other writings also have to be characterized with nuance and full recognition of the differentiated components of the whole. That is especially the case when, as I shall explain, our analytical variables appeal, in part, to the quite varied relationships between components of the Mishnah and Scripture. It becomes impossible to make a single statement of the relationship of the Mishnah to Scripture that serves to characterize all tractates. But it becomes quite possible to form groups of tractates, each set of which bears its own distinctive relationship to Scripture.

Since our interest lies in how tractates relate to Scripture, we shall adopt that criterion as our point of analytical differentiation. Simple logic dictates that, when we ask about relationships, there can be only three classes of relationship: total, none at all, and something in the middle. Here too, we can postulate as a matter of theory that a Mishnah-tractate may stand in a totally dependent relationship with Scripture, may have no relationship at all to Scripture, or may fall somewhere in between. That is a matter of theory. Now let me spell out the theory in terms of concrete facts. There are three possibilities in a relationship between a Mishnah-tractate and a passage of Scripture. First of all, Scripture supplies the topic and also provides the analytical program of the authorship of a Mishnah-tractate, chapter, or pericope. Therefore nothing within the Mishnah's treatment of the topic goes beyond the logical program of the theme Scripture provides within the details that Scripture sets forth. Second, Scripture sets forth a topic but does not then dictate the inner logic by which the topic will be worked out in a series of illustrative cases, as is the fact in the first relationship. Therefore the subject matter is scriptural, but the treatment of the subject entirely autonomous of Scripture. Third, even the subject matter is unknown to Scripture or is so casually and elliptically treated in Scripture that the Mishnah-tractate, theme and logic all together, is wholly autonomous of Scripture.

First let us consider how a Mishnah-tractate may stand in total dependence upon Scripture. Precisely what I mean by that classification requires definition, since it is not a subjective judgment. Let me give a single example of the first of the three relationships, since, from the viewpoint of the analysis of the Mishnah-tractates' agenda, that is the single operative classification. For that purpose I present first the relevant passages of Scripture, then the Mishnah's treatment of those passages. I believe it will be self-evident to readers that nothing in the Mishnah's discussion moves beyond the requirements of the exposition of the scriptural topic within the lines of analysis defined by Scripture. Here is the relevant scriptural passage, Dt. 23:25-6:

> When you go into your neighbor's vineyard, you may eat your fill of grapes, as many as you wish, but you shall not put any in your vessel. When you go into your neighbor's standing grain, you may pluck the ears with your hand, but you shall not put a sickle to your neighbor's standing grain.

This is further read in light of the statement, Dt. 25:4:

> You shall not muzzle an ox while it is threshing.

On that basis, the rule is that workers are permitted to nibble on grain or grapes on which they are working. What follows is the Mishnah's treatment of this same topic.

7:1

A.   He who hires [day] workers and told them to start work early or to stay late –

B.   in a place in which they are accustomed not to start work early or not to stay late,

C.   he has no right to force them to do so.

D.   In a place in which they are accustomed to provide a meal, he must provide a meal.

E.   [In a place in which they are accustomed] to make do with a sweet,

F.   he provides it.

G.   Everything accords with the practice of the province.

H.   M'SH B: R. Yohanan b. Matya said to his son, "Go, hire workers for us."

I.   He went and made an agreement with them for food [without further specification].

J.   Now when he came to his father, [the father] said to him, "My son, even if you should make for them a meal like one of Solomon in his day, you will not have carried out your obligation to them.

K.   "For they are children of Abraham, Isaac, and Jacob.

L.   "But before they begin work, go and tell them, '[Work for us] on condition that you have a claim on me [as to food] only for a piece of bread and pulse alone.'"

M.   Rabban Simeon b. Gamaliel says, "He had no need to specify that in so many words.

N.   "Everything [in any case] accords with the practice of the province."

7:2

A.   And these [have the right to] eat [the produce on which they work] by [right accorded to them in] the Torah:

B.   he who works on what is as yet unplucked [may eat from the produce] at the end of the time of processing;

C.   [and he who works] on plucked produce [may eat from the produce] before processing is done;

D.   [in both instances solely] in regard to what grows from the ground.

E.   But these do not [have the right to] eat [the produce on which they labor] by [right accorded to them in] the Torah:

F.   he who works on what is as yet unplucked, before the end of the time of processing;

G.   [and he who works] on plucked produce after the processing is done;

H.   [in both instances solely] in regard to what does not grow from the ground.

7:3

A.   [If] one was working with his hands but not with his feet,

B.   with his feet but not with his hands,

C.   even [carrying] with his shoulder,

D.   lo, he [has the right to] eat [the produce on which he is working].

E.   R. Yosé b. R. Judah says, "[He may eat the produce on which he is working] only if he works with both his hands and his feet."

7:4

A.   [If the laborer was working on figs, he [has] not [got the right to] eat grapes.

B.   [If he was working] on grapes, he [has] not [got the right to] eat figs.

C.   But [he does have the right to] refrain [from eating] until he gets to the best produce and then [to exercise his right to] eat.

D.   And in all instances they have said [that he may eat from the produce on which he is laboring] only in the time of work.

E.   But on grounds of restoring lost property to the owner, they have said [in addition] :

F.   Workers [have the right to] eat as they go from furrow to furrow [even though they do not then work],

G.   and when they are coming back from the press [so saving time for the employer];

H.   and in the case of an ass [nibbling on straw in its load], when it is being unloaded.

7:5

A.   A worker [has the right to] eat cucumbers, even to a denar's worth,

B.   or dates, even to a denar's worth.

C.   R. Eleazar Hisma says, "A worker should not eat more than the value of his wages."

D.   But sages permit.

E.   But they instruct the man not to be a glutton and thereby slam the door in his own face [to future employment] −

7:6

A.   A man makes a deal [with the householder not to exercise his right to eat produce on which he is working] in behalf of himself, his adult son, or daughter,

B.   in behalf of his adult manservant or womanservant,

C.   in behalf of his wife, because [they can exercise] sound judgment [and keep the terms of the agreement],

D.   But he may not make a deal in behalf of his minor son or daughter,

E.   in behalf of his minor boy servant or girl servant, or in behalf of his beast, because [they can] not [exercise] sound judgment [and keep the terms of the agreement].

What we see is a very systematic and orderly exposition of the theme, with little initiative beyond the limits of the simple logic imposed by that theme. That is to say, first, we follow the established custom, M. 7:1. Second, we define precisely what one is permitted to eat while working, M. 7:2. Third, we explain how one is permitted to take produce, and the limits of what it means to work on produce, M. 7:3. M. 7:4 then proceeds to take up interstitial cases, e.g., working on figs and eating grapes. M. 7:5, 6 ask about limits set to one's nibbling. M. 7:7 finally addresses special cases, e.g., working on produce that no one may eat.

Anyone familiar with the way in which the authorship of the Mishnah analyzes any problem or addresses any theme will find a perfectly standard program of definition and exposition, consisting of a labor of extension and limitation of the rule. While this mode of thought in general may be deemed philosophical, it bears no abstract philosophical principle, e.g., a doctrine applicable to a vast variety of cases, whether of a metaphysical or an ethical or a legal character. The mode of thought may be deemed philosophical in a rather general way, but it is not distinctive to philosophy in any limited sense by which we may define philosophy. That distinction between mode of thought and medium of thought will gain greater clarity in later parts of this study. At this point it suffices to note that the treatment of the topic at hand is simply how the Mishnah's authorship treats any topic of Scripture on which it has no particular perspective or in which it discerns no problematic external to the logic limits of the topic as Scripture sets it forth.

Second, let us consider what it means for a tractate to appear totally autonomous of Scripture, that is to say, in its entire repertoire of ideas and problems never to allude to Scripture. For that purpose I allude to a variety of tractates that take up issues that Scripture does not supply, topics Scripture does not treat, or problems Scripture does not imagine.

My first candidate is Mishnah-tractate Kelim. This tractate is wholly devoted to the exposition of problems of classification, inclusive of connection and intentionality as issues of classification.

Tractates on cleanness and uncleanness by definition form exercises of classification, since the ultimate taxa are unclean or susceptible to uncleanness and clean or insusceptible. But the exemplary power of detailed discourse to invoke fundamental principles of classification and to set forth the complexities of physics of connection is hardly exhausted by the generalizations, unclean or clean. Indeed, throughout, these form the mere result, but never the engaging problem of principled discourse. Mishnah-tractate Kelim deals with the status, as to cultic cleanness, of useful objects, tools, or utensils. Its main point is that when an object has a distinctive character, form, use, or purpose, it is susceptible to uncleanness, so that, if it is in contact with a source of uncleanness, it is deemed cultically unclean. If it is formless, purposeless, or useless, it is insusceptible. Three criteria govern the determination of what is useful or purposeful. First come properties deemed common to all utensils, whatever the material. Second are qualities distinctive to different sorts of materials. Third is the consideration of the complex purposes for which an object is made or used, primary and subsidiary, and the intention of the user is determinative. These principles generate differing formulations of problems in the unfolding of a vast tractate. None of this comes from Scripture or addresses topics or problems known to Scripture.

Other tractates with no topical dependence whatsoever on Scripture include Mishnah-tractate Berakhot, in which there is scarcely a single scriptural passage that plays a generative part in the formation of this tractate, even though some of the prayers that are recited make mention of verses of Scripture; Demai, in which not a single fact derives from Scripture; Ketubot, in which, except for Chapter Three, the factual basis is not scriptural; Moed Qatan, for which there are no pertinent verses of Scripture. Scripture knows restrictions on labor only for the opening and closing sessions of the festivals of Passover and Tabernacles, so Ex. 12:16, Lev. 23:7-8, 35-36, Num. 28:18, 25, 29:12-35; Qiddushin, for which, in the aggregate Scripture does not define the facts that form the expository center; Tohorot, of the considerations and conceptions of which Scripture knows nothing; and so forth.

To make the point simple, I conclude with reference to Mishnah-tractate Middot. Its specification of the layout and measurements of the Temple bears no clear and systematic relationship to Scripture's treatment of the same subject. Scholarship generally holds that it follows the pattern of Solomon's Temple with some adaptations of Ezekiel's, so F. J. Hollis (*The Archaeology of Herod's Temple. With a Commentary on the Tractate Middoth'* [London, 1934], p. 354), "The use made of Holy Scripture in the tractate is not such as to give the impression that somehow or other the words of Scripture are being followed...but rather that there was a fairly clear recollection of the Temple as it had been, with Holy Scripture appealed to illuminate the fact, not as authority to prove it."

The point is now clear that some tractates totally depend for the entirety of their program and analytical problematic upon Scripture, and other tractates, to begin with, address subjects or themes of which the written Torah is simply ignorant. What about the middle range? Here we come to tractates that ask of a topic supplied by Scripture questions that Scripture in no way adumbrates. Let me give three examples of what I mean. Mishnah-tractate Makhshirin forms a well-crafted essay on the interplay of intentionality and classification. The prooftexts, Lev. 11:34, 37, establish the fact of the matter, but in no way permit us to predict the problematic of the Mishnah's treatment of that topic. The order of the tractate is so worked out that each point in the development of the study of that problem is in proper place. We start with the issue of the classification of liquid, with special attention to water capable of imparting susceptibility distinguished from water not capable of doing so: the wanted, the unwanted. This forthwith invites the issue of intentionality. Then, and only then, do we proceed to the consideration of the status of water used for one purpose and water used for a subsidiary purpose, and that leads directly into the question of whether what one is assumed to desire is taken into account at all, or whether we deem evidence of prior intentionality only post facto action. So there is no way of ordering matters to produce an intelligible sequence of problems other than in the way we now have them, and this tractate is philosophical not only in its topics but in its very structure.

A second example is Mishnah-tractate Nedarim, dealing with vows, on which Scripture sets forth rules. But nearly the entire tractate addresses a philosophical problem; specifically, the authorship provides lessons in showing how species relate in a common genus, or how the components of a common genus are speciated. That is so prominent a theme that were we to want to teach the method of classification through genus and species, this is the tractate that would provide rich and exquisitely executed examples of that method. The secondary interest, not surprisingly, is in the consideration of intentionality, on the one side, and the resolution of matters of doubt, on the other. These are subordinate to the main concern of this profoundly philosophical tractate.

A third example is Mishnah-tractate Negaim, addressing Leviticus 13 and 14. This Mishnah-tractate is a deeply philosophical treatment of a subject on which Scripture has supplied a rich corpus of information. As is common in tractates on uncleanness, the basic intellectual framework is defined by problems of classification of diverse data, yielding a single outcome: unclean, clean. The classification involves hierarchization, on the one side, and the resolution of doubts as to data (never as to the pertinent rule) on the other. That is the focus of interest of the bulk of the tractate, and we find ourselves in the same realm of inquiry as in Niddah, on the one side, and Miqvaot, on the other: classification and the resolution of doubt, mostly the former. This tractate provides a splendid and compelling exemplification of the power of classification to frame and solve problems. Specifically, classification makes possible hierarchical classification, which for its part renders plausible argument on shared premises yielding firm results. The power of hierarchical classification in framing issues is shown at M. Neg. 13:10: They said to R. Judah, "If, when his entire body is unclean, he has not rendered unclean that which is on him until he will remain for a time sufficient to eat a piece of bread, when his entire body is not unclean, is it not logical that he should not render what is on him unclean until he remains for a time sufficient to eat a piece of bread?" Tosefta's reply shows what is at stake: "Said to them R. Judah, 'The reason is that the power of that which is susceptible to uncleanness also is stronger to afford protection than the power of what is insusceptible to uncleanness is to afford protection. Israelites receive uncleanness and afford protection for clothing in the house afflicted with plague, and the gentile and beast do not receive uncleanness and so do not afford protection....'" The same uses of hierarchical classification are shown at M. 13:11: "Whatever affords protection with a tightly sealed cover in the Tent of the corpse affords protection with a tightly sealed cover in the house which has a plague, and whatever affords protection merely by being covered over in the Tent of the corpse affords protection merely by being covered over in the house which has a plague," the words of R. Meir. R. Yosé says, "Whatever affords protection with a tightly sealed cover in the Tent of the corpse affords protection when merely covered over in the house which has a plague, and whatever affords protection when merely covered over in the Tent of the corpse even uncovered in the house which has the plague is clean." This argument and its numerous parallels are possible only within a system of classification in which all thought is channeled into paths of comparison and contrast, inquiries into the genus and the species and the comparison of the species of a common genus, then the hierarchization of the results, one way or another.

Enough has been said to show how readily we differentiate among the relationships between various tractates of the Mishnah and Scripture. We can now not only describe those relationships, we may also analyze and interpret them. The analysis may be appropriately brief since much that has already been said has suggested the analytical program I have devised. It is clear that where tractates are "scriptural," they merely repeat in the Mishnah's rhetoric and within the Mishnah's logic of cogent discourse what Scripture says in its rhetoric and within its logic of cogent discourse. Where tractates are not scriptural, I have now indicated, they are philosophical. This is in two aspects. An interstitial tractate – one that is scriptural in topic but not scriptural in its treatment of its topic – will ask philosophical questions of classification of a subject that Scripture has described within a different program of questions altogether. A good example of that type of interstitial tractate is Mishnah-tractate Negaim, which, as I said, wants to teach lessons of the rules of classification. Another is Mishnah-tractate Makhshirin, which proposes to investigate the relationship between one's action and the taxonomic power of one's intentionality. As to the third category, what differentiates an interstitial tractate from a completely non-scriptural tractate is simply the topic. A completely non-scriptural tractate commonly will pursue a philosophical reading of a given topic; what makes the tractate non-scriptural is the fact that Scripture does not know its topic.

In setting matters forth, I have now to indicate the proportions of the document that are scriptural, those that are (in the definition just now given) interstitial, and those that are utterly non-scriptural. Among the 61 tractates of the Mishnah, seven are neither scriptural nor philosophical (again, in terms now clear). Of the 54 others, 41 are philosophical (whether dealing with a scriptural topic or not dealing with a scriptural topic), and 13 are wholly scriptural, in the model of Yoma, for instance, or Pesahim. Of the 54 tractates that may be classified as either wholly scriptural or fundamentally philosophical, three-quarters are philosophical. Of all 61 tractates, two-thirds are philosophical. And that brings us back to the point at which we started, Rabbi Judah the Patriarch's presentation of the Mishnah as a single, seamless, internally harmonious, unitary document. To state matters simply, what Rabbi has accomplished in his formalization of the whole is the union of philosophy and revelation. I say this in a very concrete and not in an abstract sense. He has joined profound discourse on the nature of classification, the relationship of genus to species and the comparison and contrast of species, the role of intentionality in the taxonomic system, the disposition of interstitial cases in which a variety of taxic indicators come into play – Rabbi has joined a profound discourse on the nature of classification with a loving and detailed repetition of the facts of Scripture as these concern certain topics. The result is a document, the Mishnah, in which we are taught both philosophy and Scripture. Rabbi demonstrates through the Mishnah that revelation and reason, that is to say, Scripture and Mishnah's framing of philosophical principles of classification on which all knowledge rests, are shown to form a single, seamless skein of truth.

These results must strike as familiar – but also dissonant – those familiar with the great work of Moses Maimonides, the pinnacle of Jewish philosophy, who set out to do precisely what I claim Rabbi has already done in the Mishnah. For, we are all taught in our elementary lessons, Rambam wished to unite reason and revelation, Aristotle and the Torah. And, it is clear, I maintain that Rabbi has done that in the Mishnah. He has chosen an aesthetic medium for his achievement – presenting within a single rhetoric and logic the entirety of the (written) Torah, revelation and of the philosophical principles of knowledge (classification of data into intelligible patterns, discovery of the rules and logic of things) of (Aristotle's) philosophy. When we turn our attention to Maimonides, we see a different choice as to how to accomplish the same purpose, and it is a choice, we now realize, that he did not have to make. Maimonides represented revelation, the Torah, in the *Mishneh Torah,* and he further portrayed reason, philosophy, in the *Guide to the Perplexed,* each document appealing to its own aesthetic choices as to rhetoric and logic of cogent discourse. The one is modeled after the Mishnah, the other has no antecedent in the received canon of the Dual Torah to which Maimonides appealed. Accordingly, it would appear to this outsider to Maimonidean scholarship, Maimonides invented a medium for representing philosophy, preserving another medium for representing the law, and it was through the overarching intellectual system that he created that the two writings were shown to be seamless and harmonious.

If that picture, drawn by an outsider, is accurate, then we may identify a fundamental misunderstanding, on the part of Maimonides, of the character of the Mishnah, that is to say, the oral part of the one whole Torah revealed by God to Moses at Mount Sinai, and therefore of the Torah itself, and, it must follow, my ultimate goal is to correct the historic error of Maimonides, who identified Aristotle and his philosophical method as the source of correct knowledge, science, in his day. But in his misreading of the requirements of theology and philosophy of Judaism, he supposed to present philosophy outside of the framework of law, and law without sustained and specific engagement with philosophy. This came about because he did not realize the full extent to which the Mishnah, Maimonides' correct choice of the foundation document of Judaism after Scripture, stood squarely within the Aristotelian philosophical tradition.

Specifically, when Maimonides systematized philosophy in his original *Guide to the Perplexed* and law in his imitative *Mishneh Torah*, he misunderstood the fact that the law, for the Judaism of the Dual Torah, constitutes the medium for theological and philosophical reflection and expression. And that is the fact, even though at numerous specific examples, he introduced into the explanation or elucidation of the law philosophical considerations. All of these preliminary impressions await sustained clarification, but they do serve to place this project into perspective.

In his separation of the presentation of law from philosophy, he tore apart what in the Mishnah had been inextricably joined in a lasting union, which was (and is) the law of that Judaism and both its theology and also its philosophy. Seeing the law in *Mishneh Torah* as a problem merely of organization and rationalization, Maimonides did not perceive that that same law contained within itself, and fully expressed, the very same principles of theology and philosophy that in the *Guide to the Perplexed* are invoked to define what we should call Judaism. Maimonides therefore did not grasp that the law in the very document that, in his (correct) judgment contained its classic formulation, that is, the Mishnah, also set forth precisely those principles of philosophy that, in Aristotle's system as Maimonides adapted it, would frame the proposed philosophy and theology of Judaism of *The Guide to the Perplexed*. Then, in the *Guide* Maimonides (mis)represented philosophy and theology by divorcing them from their legal media of articulation, as though these could come to expression entirely outside the framework of the legal sources of Judaism. So the greatest scholar of the Mishnah of all time and the greatest Aristotelian Judaism has ever known misperceived the profound intellectual structure of the Mishnah.

The reason for this error, in my view, is that Maimonides did not understand the deeply Aristotelian character of the Mishnah, which is the initial and definitive statement of the law of Judaism. And that is the error that I am in the process of correcting in this book and in the companion studies and volumes of which it forms an offshoot and a by-product. I am showing, point by point, that the economics, politics, and philosophy, that is, the social order set forth by the Judaism of the Mishnah, finds its intellectual home in Aristotle's philosophy, method, and (in the main) results as well. The modes of thought and the basic categorical structures correspond to those of Aristotle. This has already been accomplished in my *Economics of Judaism* and *Politics of Judaism*. Now when we realize that the Mishnah stands squarely within the Aristotelian philosophical tradition in its economics, politics, and philosophical principles (a proposition, as I said, I already have shown for the first two of the three main lines of social thought), then we can understand what happened to mislead Maimonides. And from Maimonides onward, the law has served only episodically and notionally, not systematically and totally, in the formation of the theology and philosophy of Judaism. The scholars of the law in the main knew no theology and could not understand philosophy; the scholars of theology and philosophy, whether or not they knew the law, did not understand in a systematic way that the law would provide the very principles of philosophy that they thought the classic sources of Judaism did not afford. Seeing the law of Judaism, from the Mishnah forward, as essentially distinct from the philosophical science of Aristotle, Maimonides and everyone since then, if they dealt with law at all, simply arranged the law and turned to the philosophy and theology.

What Maimonides should have done, which I therefore am in the course of doing, was in a systematic and rigorous manner to show the philosophy within the law. That meant not merely that the law has or exhibits a philosophy. Everyone recognizes that simple and commonplace observation. At numerous points in his *Mishneh Torah*, Maimonides articulates the principle at hand; and, as to theology, this is encompassed within the *Mishneh Torah Sefer Ahabah*. But the fundamental modes of thought and some of the principal problems of reflection of Aristotle guide the intellectual processes of the Mishnah, and that fact Maimonides did not grasp; if he had, he would have worked out the *Guide to the Perplexed*'s main points within the very framework of legal exposition. In this way the marriage of law and philosophy, which, as a systematic program, eluded Maimonides, could have been consummated, yielding for the history of Judaism a very different result from the one that followed their divorce. For understanding the philosophical modes of thought and also the philosophical problematic of the Mishnah – issues of mixtures, issues of the potential and the actual, for instance – should have meant that the law is part of, and expresses in its distinctive idiom of rules, the rules of a well-composed and clearly defined philosophical tradition.

Not only so, but the earliest intellectual critiques of the Mishnah recognized its fundamental Aristotelianism and rejected it, as I demonstrated in *Uniting the Dual Torah: Sifra and the Problem of the Mishnah*.[1] And, as I now am showing in its principal components, that philosophical tradition in which the Mishnah stands is the very tradition that so engaged Maimonides to begin with, which is the Aristotelian one. Had he understood that fact, he would have allowed

---

[1]In press at Cambridge University Press for publication in 1990.

Aristotle to teach him philosophy through the medium of law and its structure and system. For that is precisely what Judah the Patriarch did in his presentation of the Mishnah. That is to say, through the law of the social order that the Judaism of the Dual Torah set forth Judah the Patriarch gave full and ample expression also, and at one and the same time, to philosophy and its principles and rules. What Maimonides wanted to do, Judah the Patriarch actually had accomplished a thousand years earlier – and Maimonides did not know it. That explains his mistake. When, therefore, we ask the deceptively simple question, how does the Mishnah relate to Scripture, we find ourselves addressing the most profound structural questions of the relationship of reason to revelation in the Judaism of the Dual Torah we know as normative, classical, and orthodox.

4

The Mishnah's Generative Mode of Thought: *Listenwissenschaft* and Analogical-Contrastive Reasoning

The paramount mode of reasoning in the Mishnah is what I call "analogical-contrastive reasoning." The logic may be expressed very simply: all persons, things, or actions that fall within a single species of a given genus in a uniform system of classification follow a single rule. All persons, things, or actions that fall within a different species of that same genus follow precisely the opposite rule. That reasoning by analogy and contrast dominates in the formation of the Mishnah's rules, and it is, therefore, its generative mode of thought. Through hypothetical-analytical reasoning, we can, therefore, work our way back from conclusions that the Mishnah's authorship presents through the stages of reasoning that have led to reaching those conclusions.

In an earlier chapter we have seen how the Mishnah's fundamental mode of setting forth propositions appealed to the logic and structure deriving from *Listenwissenschaft*, specifically, the logic of analogy and contrast, let me undertake a more difficult exercise. It is to prove that analogical-contrastive logic not only accounts for the document's formal traits but also explains how the document's authorship reached its conclusions, deriving from Scripture, upon which it built an entire tractate. For that purpose I turn to the conception of *maddaf*-uncleanness, which is paramount in Mishnah-tractate Zabim. Elsewhere[1] I have shown that that generative conception emerged in a process of analogy and contrast, through four successive steps, from a proposition set forth in Scripture. Here I briefly

---

[1]See my in my *History of the Mishnaic Law of Purities.* XVIII. *Zabim* (Leiden: E. J. Brill, 1977), pp. 174-192.

recapitulate the demonstration of how analogical-contrastive thinking works. The main point suffices. It is that by a simple series of steps, we can derive a concept utterly lacking in scriptural foundations, the concept of *maddaf*-uncleanness, from Scripture's explicit provision of uncleanness for persons or objects in the same status.

Maddaf-uncleanness is defined at Mishnah-tractate Zabim 5:2 as follows: "Whatever is carried above the *Zab* is unclean. And whatever the *Zab* is carried upon is clean, except for something which is suitable for sitting and lying, and except for man." To explain briefly: if food and drink, or a *maddaf*-article (which is something not used for sitting and lying) are located above the *Zab*, they are unclean, so that they impart uncleanness at one remove and unfitness at one remove. If the bed and chair bear the weight of the *Zab*, they are unclean so that they impart uncleanness at two removes and unfitness at one. Now comes the reversal. If food, drink, and *maddaf*-objects are below the *Zab*, they remain clean. What we have therefore is a set of opposites. Things a *Zab* uses for lying or sitting, as Leviticus 15:1ff. makes clear, when located beneath a *Zab* are unclean. When these same things are located above, him, they are clean. Things a *Zab* does not use for lying or sitting located beneath a *Zab* are clean; located above, they are unclean.

Not many steps in reasoning lead us from Lev. 15:10, "And whoever touches anything that was under him shall be unclean until evening," to the rule that the Mishnah presents concerning the uncleanness of certain things when located above the *Zab*. What we do is simply set forth a rule and its opposite, and do so until we reach the conception of *maddaf*-uncleanness. To begin with, if we read the verse disjunctively, then it bears the meaning that *location* of an object beneath a *Zab* – even if he is not touching it, and even if he is not riding on it – imparts uncleanness to the object. Accordingly, we take account of the spatial relationships of objects to a *Zab*. And this yields the clearly required notion that an object used for sitting, lying, or riding which is located beneath a *Zab* is unclean, even though the *Zab* has not sat, lain, or ridden on that object.

The next step is simple. Touching an object located underneath a *Zab*, even though said object is not touched by the *Zab* and even though said object is not directly sat, lain, or ridden upon by the *Zab* but merely bears the weight of his body, imparts uncleanness so that the formerly clean person is made unclean and furthermore makes his clothing unclean, and, by extension, imparts uncleanness to utensils in general. And that produces its counterpart and opposite, to be stated equally simply. It is in three parts.

First, an object used for sitting and lying which is located underneath the *Zab* is subject to the uncleanness imparted by the *Zab* to objects upon which he has sat or lain, etc. It follows that the same sort of object located above the *Zab* is *not* subject to the uncleanness imparted by the *Zab* to objects used for sitting and lying.

Second, an object not used for sitting and lying located *beneath* the *Zab* (but not touched by him or subjected to the pressure of his body-weight) is *not* unclean.

Third, it follows in the rule of opposites, an object not used for sitting and lying which is located *above* the *Zab will* be unclean in some way or degree, not specified.

Let us now relate the foregoing to M. *Zab.* 5:2. The important point is the distinction between what is carried *above* the *Zab* and what is carried *below* him, without touching him. In the former case, there is uncleanness, and this applies, specifically, to food, drink, and objects not used for lying and sitting (*maddaf*). If these are carried below the *Zab*, they are clean. Only man and bed and chair below the *Zab* are made unclean because of their serving to carry his weight even without directly touching him. The illustration, M. *Zab.* 5:2L-M, further indicates that what is unclean above the *Zab* – food, drink, *maddaf* (an object not used for lying and sitting) – is unclean in the first remove. So to recapitulate, the basic reasoning is worked out in these opposites: (1) What is unclean beneath the *Zab* is not unclean above him. (2) Then what is *not* unclean beneath the *Zab is* unclean above him. Objects not used for sitting and lying, food and drink (2) are unclean above, because they (1) are clean below, the *Zab*. Thus objects used for sitting and lying are clean above, because they are unclean below, the *Zab*.

How much of the Mishnah follows the reasoning of opposites? As we saw at the outset, in its generative mode of thought, the authorship compares the species of a genus, assigning to all items on one list the same rule, and to all items on the opposed list, the opposite rule. So analogical-contrastive reasoning lies at the foundation of *Listenwissenschaft*. Where the process just now set forth proves especially interesting is where we wish to move from two known poles, Scripture's rule, the Mishnah's law, toward the unknown range between them. Here is the point at which we can propose through a series of steps of opposite positions to reconstruct how people reasoned, from the one pole to the other. Not only so, but the exercise in theoretical reasoning conducted with reference to the (scriptural) origins of *maddaf*-uncleanness can readily be repeated, as the case requires, for the principles and generative rules of three tractates, Negaim, Niddah, and the remainder of Zabim, all of which to begin with draw out and spell out Scripture's rules and principle for the *mesora'*, the menstruating woman, *Zabah,* woman after childbirth, and finally, for the *Zab,* respectively.

The logic of analogical-contrastive thinking will account for every detail of the rules that to begin with are not simply paraphrases of what we find in Scripture. This hypothetical-logical explanation of the working of *Listenwissenschaft* places the Mishnah's mode of reasoning square within the scientific-philosophical tradition of the ancient Near East even in most remote antiquity.[2]

---

[2]Compare G. E. R. Lloyd, *Polarity and Analogy. Two Types of Argumentation in Early Greek Thought* (Cambridge: Cambridge University Press, 1966). The core-logic of *Listenwissenschaft* extends back to Sumerian times. But in my *The Philosophy of Judaism. The First Principles* (in progress) I shall show that the immediate context of this mode of natural philosophy is in the Second Sophistic.

5

Why an Economics in the Judaism of the Dual Torah

Some religions set forth doctrines of economics, and others do not. Knowing why a religious system appeals to economics or politics in the composition of its system – its way of life, worldview, and theory of the social entity that realize that way of life and worldview – tells us about the uses of politics or economics that secular social systems do not. While we can well understand why any social system must deal with the questions addressed by politics and economics, it is not equivalently obvious why religious systems must or may do so. For politics deals with the legitimate use of coercion, including violence, and economics with the rational disposition of scarce resources. Religion is commonly understood to eschew violence, and whatever religion has to say about the disposition of scarce resources is ordinarily assumed to be known: give it all to the poor, for instance.

Yet at a critical moment the Judaism of the Dual Torah, beginning with Scripture and then the Mishnah, a philosophical system in the form of a law code formed at about 200 C.E., found it necessary to formulate its system by providing an elaborate picture of both economics and politics. And that picture of the disposition of scarce resources, on the one side, and the legitimate uses of violence, on the other, formed an absolutely fundamental medium for expressing the larger systemic message that that Judaism proposed to set forth. What makes that fact interesting is that, in the same time and place, Christianities, taking shape in a variety of systems, in no way followed suit. That is to say, we cannot identify a Christian system – a way of life, worldview, theory of the Christian society – that appeals to economics and politics for its systemic formation and statement. While the New Testament and other early Christian writings here and there make statements about subjects classified as economic or political, these writings in no way lay out what we can call an economics or a politics. But the Judaic writings did. I want to ask, in particular, why was there an economics in that Judaism?

The explanation for that contrast does not lie in the fact that Christians had no state, while Jews did. In fact, for more than a hundred years prior to the closure of the Mishnah, there had been no Jewish state, and the Jews' status as a corporate political entity was hardly formidable. Nor can we point to the Jews' memory of a Jewish state, such as the Hebrew Scriptures portray, since, after all, Christians appealed to that same Scripture and made their own that same memory of a sacred politics. Indeed, the representation of Jesus as a political figure, the appeal in particular to the political metaphor of Christ the King, the claim that Jesus was supposed to be, or have been, the king of the Jews – all of this invited the formation of a Christian politics. And in due course there would be both a Christian politics and also a Christian economics. But there was none prior to Augustine (if then), and, so far as economics is concerned, we have to await the Christianization of Aristotle, including Aristotle's economics, for the true formation of an economics of Christianity and within Christianity.

All of this comes so much later in the history of Christianity as to make still more urgent the question, why is it that a particular Judaism found in economics a medium for systemic composition, while no Christianity did? The answer must come first in the explanation of why this? and then we can attempt also to consider, why not that? Let me start from the beginning, with a simple observation. It is that the world-construction, Judaism, as portrayed by the Mishnah, encompasses all subjects that pertain to the life of an entire nation and society. Such a program of world-construction by its nature involves three principal intellectual tasks of theoretical thought, politics, economics, and science or learning. A system that proposes to set forth the main frame and structure of a society will commonly make its statement in what it says about all three matters, establishing the same fundamental principle or viewpoint or attitude in treating each critical component of its theory of the social system. That basic harmony and coherence in what is said by a system about economics, politics, and science will ordinarily characterize a well-composed theory of world-construction. Economics is systemically not inert but active and generative, indeed expressive of the basic message of the system of the Mishnah as a whole.

A theory of economics forms an integral and coherent component of the larger theoretical statement of a social system. For no utopian design, such as is given by the Mishnah, a classic political novel or

Staatsroman in the tradition of Plato's *Republic* and Aristotle's *Politics,* can ignore the material organization of society. True, in modern times we are accustomed to view economics as disembedded from the political and social system, the market, for instance, as unrelated to kinship or institutions of culture. But until the eighteenth century economics was understood as a component of the social system, and also a formative constituent of culture. It follows that those religious systems, such as Judaism, Islam, and Christianity in its medieval phase, that propose to prescribe public policy in the earthly city and design a social world will integrate into their systems theories of (correct) economic behavior and also accounts of systemically correct economic policy. Then precisely how does a religion make its systemic statement, also, through its economics?

Economics today is defined as the theory of rational action with regard to scarcity. The economics of the Mishnah was a mode of rational action with regard to scarcity. That the document portrays an economics within its larger system cannot be doubted, for the Mishnah treats subjects ordinarily addressed in antiquity by documents generally deemed to bear upon issues of economics and does so within the economic theory of Aristotle. Like Aristotle's economics, the Mishnah's economics is a thorough-going, distributive economics which at the same time recognized the presence also of a market economics. For in the theory of the Mishnah both the market and the distributive systems form one system and represent two components of one system. So we deal with a single theory holding together two distinct economics. But the distributive component of the Mishnah's economic theory is the effective part. It is what reshapes the three principal categories of economic thought in that time and place, namely, the household, the market, and wealth. Why did the system of the Mishnah appeal to a distributive economics? The answer to that question comes to us from theology, not economics. What the Mishnah's authorship wished to say, we shall now see, they could express only by utilizing the principal categories of economics I just mentioned.

The economics of the system has been shaped by the larger systemic statement and message The Mishnah's is, in fact, a theology that comes to expression in the details of material transactions. For the Mishnah's distributive economics derives from the theory that the Temple and its scheduled castes on earth exercise God's claim to the ownership of the holy land. At the center of the Mishnah's economics is the disposition of resources with unremitting regard to the status of recipients in the transaction. Who are the parties to the system? We begin with God, the principal economic partner of whom is the Israelite farmer. God owns the earth. But the particular earth that God owns is the Land of Israel, and, within that land, the particular earth is land in the Land of Israel that is owned by an Israelite. With that Israelite, a land-owner in the Land of Israel, God is co-owner. From that theological principle, spun out of the notion that when Israelites occupy the land that God has given to the Israelites, namely, the Land of Israel, that land is transformed, and so too are the principles of ownership and distribution of the land, all else flows.

The economics of the Judaism rests upon the theory of the ownership of a designated piece of real estate, ownership that is shared between God and partners of a certain genus of humanity whose occupancy of that designated piece of real estate, but no other, affects the character of the dirt in question. The theology consists in an account of what happens when ground of a certain locale is subject to the residency and ownership of persons of a certain genus of humanity. The generative conception of the theology involves a theory of the affect – the enchantment and transformation – that results from the intersection of "being Israel:" land, people, individual person alike.

Since God owns the Land of Israel, God – represented by, or embodied through, the Temple and priesthood and other scheduled castes – joins each householder who also owns land in the Land of Israel as an active partner, indeed, as senior partner, in possession of the landed domain. God not only demands a share of the crop, hence comprises a householder. God also dictates rules and conditions concerning production, therefore controls the householder's utilization of the means of production. Furthermore, God additionally has provided as a lasting inheritance to Israel, the people, the enduring wealth of the country which is to remain stable and stationary and not to change hands in such wise that one grows richer, the other poorer. Every detail of the distributive economics therefore restates that single point: *the earth is the Lord's.* That explains why the householder is partner of the Lord in ownership of the land, so that the Lord takes his share of the crop at the exact moment at which the householder asserts his ownership of his portion.

But the ongoing partnership between God and Israel in the sanctification and possession of the land is not a narrowly secular arrangement. Both parties share in the process of the sanctification of the land, which accounts for, and justifies, Israel's very possession of the land. The Israelite landowner has a particular role in effecting the sanctification of the land, in that, land is holy and subject to the rules of God only when the Israelite landowner owns land in the Land of Israel. Once more, land located elsewhere owned by Israelites, and land located in the Land of Israel but not owned by Israelites, has no material relationship to the processes of sanctification, in utilization and in the disposition of the products of the land, that are at the heart of the distributive economics at hand. In the conception of the authorship of the Mishnah, therefore, all land was held in joint tenancy, with the householder as one partner, God as the other. That mixed ownership then placed side by side two economic systems, one distributive, resting on control of property by the Temple acting in behalf of the owner of the land, who was god, the other the market system in which private persons owned property and with legal sanction could use it and transfer title without intervention from any other power.

We have now to identify that component of the goods and services of the market that is subjected to distributive, rather than market, economics, within the mixed economics at hand. It is, in particular, food that is subjected to the distributive system at hand – food and, in point of fact, nothing else, certainly not capital, or even money. Manufactured goods and services, that is, shoes on the last, medical and educational services, the services of clerks and scribes, goods in trade, commercial ventures of all kinds – none of these is subjected to the tithes and other sacerdotal offerings. The possibility of the mixed economics, market and distributive alike, rests upon the upshot of the claim that God owns the holy land. It is the land that God owns, and not the factory or shop, stall and store, ship and wagon, and other instruments and means of production. Indeed, the sole unit of production for which the Mishnah legislates in rich and profound exegetical detail is the agricultural one. The distributive component of the economy, therefore, is the one responsible for the production of food, inclusive of the raising of sheep, goats, and cattle. Again, the centerpiece is ownership of land. What does not derive from the earth owned jointly by God and the Israelite householder falls outside the economics of Judaism in its initial statement.

Wealth consists of land and what land produces, crops and cattle, as well as a large labor force, comprising the children of a growing population. The link of fertility to tithing occurs at Dt. 14:22-29, in connection with the separation of the tithe and the delivery of the tithe to Jerusalem, where it is to be eaten by the householder: "that the Lord your God may bless you in all the work of your hands that you do." "Proper disposition of the tithe...will result in God's blessing of the soil and its increased productivity." The conception that wealth is solely land, is expressed not only in rules for the householder but also in silence: tithe derives only from herds and agricultural produce. The artisan and craftsman, the personnel of the service economy, merchants and traders and other commercial persons – none of these has anything to tithe. While they may have possessed wealth in the form of goods and even money, the distributive economics of the Mishnah had no rules governing the disposition of that wealth, which was left without recognition. And yet, as we have seen, the market economics of the Mishnah made ample provision for the governance of wealth in other forms than real estate. On that basis – the awry theory of wealth – I maintain the Mishnah presents, side by side, two distinct theories of economics, the one a market economics, the other, a more familiar distributive economics. But once more we enter the caveat: the Mishnah's economics is distributive, but it makes provision for an economics of a market enclave as well. So the theories are distinct but not dual, not correlative.

At the end we have to listen not only to what the authorship of the Mishnah says, but also to what it does not treat. In fact, the economics of the system expresses in tacit omissions a judgment concerning the dimensions of the economy that to begin with falls subject to the enchantment of sanctification expressed in glorious triviality by our authorship. For matching the explicit rules are the authorship's ominous silences. Its land-centeredness permits its economics to have no bearing either on the economy comprising Jews who were not householders, nor on Jews who lived overseas. The Mishnah's distributive economics is for the "Israel" of "the Land of Israel" to which the Mishnah speaks. There is no address to the economics of "Israel" outside of the land. For distributive economics governs only agricultural produce of the Land of Israel, and, it follows, market economics is tacitly assigned as the mode of distribution for everything else and is operative everywhere else. No wonder, then, that the framers of the Talmud of Babylonia, addressing, as they did, Jews who did not live on holy or sanctified dirt, took no interest whatsoever in the Mishnah-tractates upon which we have focused here, the ones that state in rich detail the theory of a distributive economics of God as owner, scheduled caste as surrogate, Temple as focus, and enlandisement as rationale, for an utterly fictive system.

For the framers of the Mishnah maintained that scarcity represented Heaven's judgment upon the condition of the nation, and, therefore, to prevent scarcity one had to secure the favor of Heaven. The things that became scarce when Heaven was displeased had properly to be arrayed before and transported to Heaven through the heavens. And these things were the product of the earth, the fields and farms, the herds and vineyards and orchards. Heaven governed these things, and so in order to avoid scarcity, heaven's rules had to be observed, a conception brought down to this morning's labor by appeal to God as joint-holder and joint-owner of the land along with the Israelite owner of the land in the Land of Israel in particular. Not only so, but when scarcity affected the nation, or classes within the nation, that same mode of arraying goods and transporting them dictated what was to be done rationally to deal with scarcity. So faced with a set of choices about the disposition of scarce goods, the authorship of the Mishnah made entirely rational decisions on how to make use of the goods and services of the economy in such a way as to prevent scarcity by removing its cause, on the one side, and to deal with scarcity when it made itself affective and even dangerous, on the other.

A full account, therefore, of the economics of the Mishnah as a rational program of dealing with scarcity requires us to enter into the rationality of the system as a whole, for, we now realize, the parts of the system that concern economics form an integral component of the statement of that large, whole worldview and way of life that, all together, constituted the Judaism of the formative document under study. Through the system of the Mishnah at each of its principal constituents, sages say pretty much the same things about the world of nature and supernature which they express in the other divisions of the Mishnah. What is that point of emphasis? At point after point in their system, the framers of the Mishnah declare the one conviction that the Israelite world – Jews in Palestine/Israelites in the Land of Israel – forms a world unto itself, a world order of enduring stasis, in which no significant change will disturb the stable society. This world-order, down below, attains that enduring, indeed, eternal stasis because it serves down here to complement and complete the other world-order, the one in Heaven. In the complementarity and wholeness attained through the union of two opposites – Heaven and earth – on the sacred time of the Sabbath and festivals, creation is renewed, and, on that account, creation in all its completeness and perfection once more provokes in God the benediction and sanctification of the Creator such as the original excellence of creation had elicited.

This absolutely fundamental conviction comes to concrete expression in diverse ways. The one within economics emphasizes the true, intrinsic worth and value of things, the perfect balance in transactions, so that each party to an exchange, conceived as equal barter, gets worth equivalent to what he gives, and both parties emerge precisely at the same level of worth as they had at the outset. But that conception of the perfection of the steady-state economy is only one way in which the systemic principle comes to statement in the details of everyday exchange. To give one example of how in other ways the conception of the basically stationary character of the world order reaches concrete expression, we turn to politics. Specifically, what the Israelite government is supposed to do for its part also is to preserve that state of perfection that society everywhere attains and expresses in economic and other material transactions as well. People are to follow and maintain the prevailing practice of their locale. The purpose of civil penalties is to restore the injured party to his prior condition, so far as this is possible, rather than merely to penalize the aggressor. So there is no surprise that the system invoked economic theory in order to make its statement.

In a perfect society (as perfection is understood by our mishnaic philosophers) true value means that a given object has an intrinsic worth, which in the course of a transaction must be paid. And, for that same reason, we introduce the topic of usury which, we noted, sages treated as integral to the conception of "fraud" as the violation of true value. There can be no such thing as usury, which means essentially profit. Any pretense that money increases or has become more than what it was violates the conception of true value. When real estate is divided, it must be done with full attention to the rights of all concerned, so that one party does not gain at the expense of the other. In these and many other aspects the law of the Mishnah expresses its obsession with the perfect stasis and enduring order of Israelite society. Its paramount purpose is in preserving and insuring that that perfection of the division and order of this world is kept inviolate or restored to its true status when violated. And that systemic message required attention to economics, not because the subject matter was necessary to a full and encompassing statement of the social order, for other world-constructions made their statements of the right construction and composition of the social order without addressing economics at all. It was because only by addressing the *theory* of economics, the received distributive theory adapted to the Mishnah's purposes and subjected to exquisite amplification and extension in the exegesis of the Mishnah's authorship, could the systemic program reach full realization. That is why the Mishnah presents an economics.

But the economics of the Mishnah is not an economics at all. The reason is that, as I have explained, in the Mishnah's system, economics is embedded in an encompassing structure, to which economic considerations are subordinated, forming merely instrumental components of a statement made not in response to, but merely through, economics. And economics can emerge as an autonomous and governing theory only when disembedded from politics and society. Economic institutions, such as the market, the wage system, a theory of private ownership, and the like, in no way can have served the system of the Mishnah. The reason is not that in their moral or ethical value they proved less, or more, suitable than competing institutions. These would have been, for example, such as the sacerdotal system of production and distribution, a theory of divine-human joint tenancy, and a system made up of both wages for labor and also fees for correct genealogy, that the Mishnah's framers adopted. Economics viewed in its own terms cannot have served the system of the Mishnah because the system-builders viewed nothing in its own terms, but all things in the framework of the social system they proposed to construct. I earlier observed that Christian theologians for the first seven centuries simply ignored economics, having no theory to contribute to economic thought and no sustained interest in the subject. But when we realize the character and function of economics in the system of the Mishnah, we realize that the same reason accounts for the presence of an economics as for its absence.

The way forward leads us to Max Weber's insistence that the correct point of analysis of a system, therefore comparison and contrast of system to system, is in the description, analysis, and interpretation of the rationality of the system, then the comparison of rationality to rationality. Marx's reading is simply beside the point. For if we cannot explain the economic theory of a system by reference only to class interest and class struggle, then what makes the system work is some other generative component than class interest and class struggle. In the case of the Mishnah, class-status seems to me to compete with class interest and therefore to form a negative force in the working out of what the Marxists must conceive to be the class struggle. True, class-status, the comparison of the householder in particular to God in particular, can have valued economic consequences. But in the system before us, the opposite is the fact. The economic interests of the householder contradict the requirements of class-status for reasons I have specified time and again. That is why I find the rationality of the system elsewhere than in those considerations of class structure and class struggle that to Marxists appeared prominent and even determinative. To the forces of class structure and class struggle, my analysis has taught me to counterpose the considerations of systemic rationality.

Economics, nonetheless, defines an important component of the rationality of a social system aiming at the construction of a society. And that is why, if we are to compare the rationality of one system to the rationality of some other, we also have to learn how to compare economics to economics, political economy to political economy. This mode of analysis – comparison and contrast – demands us even to know *which* component of a given system serves as the counterpart and corresponding component to the economics of another system, beginning, of course, with our own. And that explains the larger program of the inquiry now concluded. For I have addressed – in a very particular framework – the question of translating from one culture to another the theory of economics, that is, rational action in regard to scarcity, and, in a subsidiary sense, also to the increase and disposition of wealth. By describing the economics of a world different from our own, I mean ultimately to penetrate into the meaning of rationality, encompassing rational action in matters of scarcity and also wealth, its increase and disposition, in a universe other than the familiar one of the secular West.

To do so, we cannot simply adopt and apply to an alien world that contemporary and commonplace theory of economics that for us describes and accounts for the rationality of economic action. That would tell us nothing about rational economic action in a world in which rationality bears different rules from the ones we know. Rather, we have to identify within that other world, different from our own, the things that to them fell into the category we know as economic. Specifically, we ask, what are the things they regarded as rational actions in regard to scarcity, and also to matters of wealth, its increase and disposition? And how did they uncover hypotheses of rationality in economic action and test them and translate them into rules of intelligent economic action? In this way we do not merely adopt, but adapt the issues of economics by allowing for economic action to follow rules different from the ones we know yet to accord with conceptions we nonetheless can claim to understand. In asking our questions about economics – theory of rational action in the face of scarcity and in the increase and disposition of wealth – we discern and, I think, in context understand alien answers to those same familiar questions. Our rationality thus constructs a program of inquiry into the rationality concerning common issues, differently sorted out, by different people, in a different world from our own. In that way we aim to enter into, and understand, someone else's economic rationality, and so, too, someone else: another person. That seems to me the task of the social study of religion – but also the highest ambition of religion.

6

Why Politics in Judaism?

Inquiry into the ancient state and government needs to be lowered from the stratosphere of rarefied conceptions, by a consideration not only of ideology, of 'national' pride and patriotism, of *der staat,* of the glories and miseries of war, but also of the material relations among the citizens or classes of citizens as much as those more commonly noticed between the state and the citizens.

M. I. Finley[1]

There is an interesting disjuncture between the Mishnah's economics and its politics. The householder is the building block of the house of Israel, of its *economy* in the classic sense of the word, but the politics of the house of Israel does not know him. But if there is a disjuncture between the generative metaphor of the Mishnah's economics and the one that is spun out in its politics, the systemic message is the same in both cases. And the same reason for a systemic economics accounts for its inclusion of a politics as well. When we can explain why the one, we understand also the reason for the other. The message of the document as a whole concerns order and stability, and that means, hierarchization of things and persons in proper place and order. The one thing the Mishnah does not want to tell us is about change, how things come to be what they are. The Mishnah's pretense is that all of these have come to rest. What do we learn from the difference between Aristotle's and the Mishnah's politics, about the Mishnah's system of the social order?

Through politics, sages registered a point that far transcended the subjects at hand. That point addresses the relations among classifications of persons and the relationships among those

---

[1]M. I. Finley, *Politics in the Ancient World* (Cambridge: Cambridge University Press, 1983), p. 49.

classifications.[2]   These relations, while transcending the matter of
legitimate violence, encompassed the politics though within a larger
frame.   That fact explains why the Mishnah's particular Judaism
invoked politics in making its larger statement.   The system required a
politics because an important part of its message in the system-builders'
judgment could come to expression only in a politics.   The question
therefore is, what was that message, and why was politics, in
particular, the correct medium for stating it?   One might wish to argue
that it was perfectly natural for a Judaism to formulate a politics.
Politics was a choice made available by the ancient Israelite
Scriptures, since the character of the pentateuchal system assuredly
found definition in the establishment of an "Israel" fully empowered,
and fully enlandised as well.   But while philosophers in Greco-Roman
times routinely addressed political issues, framers of Judaisms and
Christianities did not.   As a matter of fact, other Judaisms and
Christianities set forth their systemic program in entire indifference to
the issues of politics.   And this point requires serious consideration, so
that the issue before us – why a politics at all – will gain its rightful
weight.

The topical program of the Mishnah, when compared with the
themes deemed urgent by other system-builders of the Judaisms and
Christianities of the time, is unique in its sustained and systematic
interest in civil law and government.   There is in the writings of other
Judaisms simply no counterpart to the design for an everyday and
functioning political structure and system.   The profoundly political
character of this Judaism becomes astonishing when we look at the
writings of the earliest Christian figures, both in the Gospels and in
the Letters of Paul, for instance.   There we search in vain for any
political discourse whatsoever, one that might bear implications for
political institutions and their operation.   To Jesus are attributed
sayings that respond to political facts, but none that will frame such
facts; Paul is utterly apolitical.   Indeed, sayings cited in Jesus' name
argue against any Christian politics whatsoever.   And that conforms to
a familiar fact, that the earliest writings of Christianity hardly
contain the raw materials for political theory of any kind; the exercise
of power lies beyond the imagination of the Christian system-builders
and thinkers even after the advent of Constantine.   From the formation
of the Mishnah, ca. 200, two centuries would pass before a Christian
writer would set forth a political theory of ambition and weight.   But

---

[2]I avoid the word "classes," because that bears meanings hardly demonstrated
to be present here.   Finley's writings on class and class structure in antiquity
seem to me the model to be followed.

the parallel with the politics of Judaism in initial context even then is inexact. For Augustine, the first Christian political thinker, did his work well after Christianity had for a long time gained the standing of a political power, and in its name Christian emperors and bishops alike for more than a century had wielded power and enjoyed the right of exercising legitimate violence.

If a system of Christianity, such as Augustine set forth, encompassed a politics, it was because Christianity by nature of its institutional position formed a political power within the Roman empire. That did not make it necessary for Augustine to think up a politics for his Christianity, but it made it plausible and natural to do so.[3] But the authorship of the Mishnah, remembering a Jewish state perhaps, never knew what it meant to put a person to death for a felony, nor did they take away people's property in the name of collecting taxes, nor did they beat, nor did they maim, nor did they expel and send anyone into exile, all in the name of the legitimate rule of the law enforced by the legally constituted and just state. Augustine was a bishop; he knew what power was. The sages of the Mishnah, if they held any power at all, were at best local busybodies: from the perspective of competing figures mere meddlers and no-accounts and bunglers, pretending to make up their minds and bear weighty opinions about matters of which, in point of fact, they were utterly without experience. Why a political Judaism? To address that question, we turn the question to philosophy: why a philosophy that attends, also, to politics?

The task of identifying the role of politics in the systemic composition, and defining the unique message that was assigned to politics by the system, now is clear. We do well to begin with the judgment of the great M. I. Finley concerning the uses of politics by Aristotle: "In the *Politics* Aristotle defined man as a *zoon politikon*, and what that meant is comprehensible only in the light of his metaphysics; hence correct translation requires a cumbersome paraphrase – man is a being whose highest goal, whose *telos* (end) is by nature to live in a *polis*."[4] It follows that sustained and cogent thought on politics, in particular, formed a critical component of Aristotle's larger thought on the nature of humanity. Political science encompasses all other areas of learning:

---

[3] I do not claim that that is why he did so. My intent is only to contrast Augustine's situation with that of the Mishnah's authorship.

[4] M. I Finley, *Politics in the Ancient World* (Cambridge: Cambridge University Press, 1983), p. 25.

Now since political science uses the rest of the sciences, and since, again, it legislates as to what we are to do and what we are to abstain from, the end of this science must include those of the other sciences, so that its end must be the good for man.[5]

If Aristotle wishes to discuss "the whole of human good," he must address a politics, and, as Mulgan states at the outset of his exposition, "An account of Aristotle's political theory must therefore begin with his conception of human good."[6]

Let us dwell for a moment on how politics delivers the systemic message concerning human good. Aristotle starts with a definition of "human good" meaning "the good life." What are the traits of happiness? "The happy man will be someone who values the philosophical contemplation of eternal truths above all else and will devote a considerable amount of his time to it."[7] And again, Mulgan states, "The subject matter of political science is human action."[8] Aristotle's main purpose in the *Politics* is...to provide a handbook of guide for the intending statesman; "political science" is also "statesmanship."[9] Aristotle is writing primarily for the ruler, "the statesman or legislator who will be making important political decisions, rather than for the ordinary citizen; his political science is statesmanship not civics."[10] And what is it that Aristotle wishes to accomplish through his political philosophy? "The overtly practical purpose of Aristotle's political science explains the close dependence of the *Politics* on his conception of human good. Political decisions must be based not only on knowledge about the workings of politics but also on some view of the ends of goals which the community ought to be pursuing."[11] The starting point for Aristotle, then, is the goals which the statesman ought to achieve; next will certainly come generalizations or rules about how these goals are to be achieved in different types of political situations; finally the rules will be applied to actual situations.[12] The role of political thought in the definition of human good, therefore, is critical:

The happy man will be someone who values the philosophical contemplation of eternal truths above all else and will devote a

---

[5]Mulgan, *Politics of Aristotle*, p. 3.
[6]*Ibid.*, p. 3.
[7]*Ibid.*, p. 6.
[8]*Ibid.*, p. 8.
[9]*Ibid.*
[10]*Ibid.*, p. 9.
[11]*Ibid.*
[12]*Ibid.*, pp. 10-11.

considerable amount of his time to it....This conception of the good life provides the background and inspiration for most of Aristotle's political theory. The connection between his ethical ideals and his political science is most clearly expressed in the last chapter of the Ethics, where, having completed his account of the good life, he raises the question of now it is to be implemented. People are unlikely to become good unless the government and the laws are directed toward the achievement of human good. The complete 'philosophy of human nature' must therefore include the study of laws and constitutions and how best to frame them....The influence of Aristotle's ethics on his politics will be most apparent in his discussion of the nature of the polis and in his account of the ideal state which is intended to implement the ethical ideal.[13]

Accordingly, Aristotle attends to political science because he is interested in the nature of the human being and especially in human action.

That fact explains why politics forms a medium for the expression of his larger system of thought on the nature of the human being and human society. The principal point is that the politics of Aristotle forms part of a larger inquiry into how things are by nature. In this connection we rapidly review what formed the centerpiece of our inquiry into the role of the household in Aristotle's *polis.* Aristotle's philosophical program, we remember, is to investigate what accords with nature or exists by nature. In this context the correct mode of thought derives from the discovery and classification of the traits and characteristics of things by nature. So Mulgan: "Because this world is constructed according to a coherent and rational pattern, it is proper...that each species should develop and exercise its own natural characteristics. By doing so, it realizes its 'essence' and performs its work of function."[14] The appeal to nature, beginning with biology and ending with the political community, then accounts for the place of the politics in the larger system, to which politics likewise proves natural and necessary. The subject matter accounted for, the message delivered through this topic as through many others spelled out, we may now turn to the counterpart for the initial Judaism.

When we come to Judaism and ask, what is the message of politics, and why does politics serve as a particularly appropriate medium for the message? we do best to begin with not similarity but difference. For having established grounds for comparison, we now explore the incongruities of the two systems. Each seen in this light will then serve through the outline of its shadow to highlight the indicatively

---

[13]*Ibid.,* p. 6.
[14]*Ibid.,* p. 18.

different, systemic traits of the other. I find the most striking difference in the locative character of power in Aristotle's system, the utopian locus of power in the Mishnah's. Judaism's politics really is a politics of nowhere in particular, by which I mean, Jerusalem and anywhere else without differentiation.[15] The *polis* is not an operative category, nor the village and its constituent households for that matter, because these are just not of consequence. Politics in Judaism takes place anywhere anyhow.

That difference is profound because it accounts for the utterly incommensurate categories of social discourse characteristic of the two systems' respective politics. That fact prepares us to recognize that the systemic message of the initial Judaism has made of the topic, politics, something quite particular. From the different choices as to the irreducible, minimal building blocks different constructions arise. Then where shall we begin in our effort to explore difference? To understand the message for which politics served as a medium, and to explain why that particular medium uniquely served the purposes of the system-builders, we return to our discussion of the systemic myth, spun out of the facts of power in its most brutal political form, from which, after all, all else flows.

Now we are prepared to take up our final questions: why a political Judaism? and what message did this Judaism express uniquely, or most powerfully, in the medium of a fabricated political structure and system? The principal message of politics in the system of Judaism derives, we recall, from our capacity to differentiate among the applications of power by reference to the attitude of the person who comes into relationship with that power. We remember that if the deed is deliberate, then one institution among the set of politically empowered institutions exercises jurisdiction and utilizes supernatural power. If the deed is inadvertent, another political agency exercises jurisdiction and utilizes the power made available by that same

---

[15]On the surface, both the economics and the politics take up issues of place. The economics of the Mishnah is profoundly locative, in line with the simple fact that the concerns of householders are in transactions in land. Their measurement of value is expressed in acreage of top, middle, and bottom grade. Through real estate critical transactions are worked out. The marriage settlement depends upon real property. Civil penalties are exacted through payment of real property. The principal transactions to be taken up are those of the householder who owns beasts which do damage or suffer it; who harvests his crops and must set some of them aside, and so by his own word and deed sanctify them for use by the castes scheduled from on high; who uses or sells his crops and feeds his family; and who, if he is fortunate, will acquire still more land. None of this has any bearing upon the politics of the document. But the interest of politics in place – Jerusalem in particular – cannot be by-passed.

supernatural being. Where a system differentiates, there it delivers its critical message. So the point at which the system tells us, why this, not that? marks the exegetical fulcrum of the system. And that, we recall, lies in the systemic identification of the two powers that do conflict, God's and the human person's. The entire politics works out the issues of power that to begin with are generated out of that conflict. And, by the way, the politics then identifies political agencies to deal with the several distinct types of conflict between those two wills.

The entire message of the system is contained within that resolution of the competition of the power of will: hierarchization, beginning at the very foundations of all being. The question answered by the politics for the system, and by the system as a whole, is this: what happens when God's will, which is supreme, confronts conflict ("rebellion," "sin," "disobedience") with the human will, which is subordinate? And the answer is, God's will be done, and this – this politics – is how. Why politics? Because the system recognizes that the human will does constitute power. It is, moreover, power to be reckoned with, taken into account, deemed legitimate even in its violent confrontation with God. And therefore – because of its very legitimacy – the power formed of the human will is to be met with equal, and equally legitimate, violence that the political system, acting in God's behalf, effects. The hierarchization of power sets forth the systemic problem, and the theory of the politics of Judaism defines the self-evidently valid solution.

The conflict worked out by politics, then, is between God's will, expressed in the law of the Torah, and the human being's will, carried out in obedience to the law of the Torah or in defiance of that law. Here, as we noted in the beginning, is a reprise of the politics of Eden: the conflict between God's power and humanity's power, which is to say, between God's commandment and humanity's freedom to obey or to disobey. The politics of Judaism emerges as a reprise, in stunning detail, of the story of God's commandment, humanity's disobedience, God's sanction for the sin or crime, and humanity's atonement and reconciliation. When Adam and Eve exercise their own will and defy God, they set their power, consisting in free choice to obey or disobey, against God's power, consisting in the capacity to command – but to command without coercion. And because of that limitation, it is a conflict of wills that stand in equal contest with one another, humanity's and God's. That again forms the systemic question: how to order equal powers? The power of the will of the one against the strength of the will of the other (a will limited by self-restraint, to be sure) forms not so much the theme of the system before us as its problematic. That, in my view, accounts for the system's profound engagement with issues of hierarchization. The dynamic of the system derives from the capacity of human attitude and intention to define culpable action, and, as I said, that central theme draws us back to the myth of Adam and Eve in Eden. Once more we note the principal message: God commands, but humanity does what it then chooses. In the interplay of those two protean forces, each a power in its own right, the sanctions and penalties of the system apply.

Why did this Judaism find a politics necessary, why was a political statement integral, and what statement did Judaism make through its politics? Politics served because politics expresses in a concrete way the theory of the disposition of power. This Judaism wished to work out the relationship between the power of God to command and the power of humanity freely to obey or disobey. But what, in connection with the abstraction power, drew attention? It was the means of sorting out whose power matters and under what circumstances. The statement of the politics before us, drawn from the mythic foundation of the entire structure, concerns divine power mediated by the criterion of the effects of the human will among three media of divine intervention: the Heavenly court above, earthly court below, Temple altar in between. Power, as we noted earlier, works its way in the interplay between what God has set forth in the law of the Torah and what human beings do, whether intentionally, inadvertently, obediently, or defiantly. Accordingly, a politics was necessary, a political statement integral, to Judaism. And given the subject matter of politics, the legitimate uses of coercion, we may hardly find astonishing the inclusion, in the initial Judaism, of a politics.

But what was the shape of the particular statement that emerged? To answer that question, we turn from the myth to the method: how, precisely, did the sages of the Mishnah work out their politics? When we know the answer to that encompassing question, we shall understand the character of the system's details, just as when we know the main purpose of Aristotle's system, we can also account for the character of his fictive politics. That is why the answer to that question draws us to an account of Judaism's counterpart to Aristotle's thesis about the priority of the natural over the conventional, his insistence upon the principle, prior to all propositions, that institutions, whether political or otherwise, derive from the very nature of things and serve to realize the potential that is inherent in that nature, are justified by the traits of human nature. Accordingly, here we shall juxtapose and compare things that, when we began this inquiry, cannot have appeared to us to be either congruent or – as we shall see in a moment – even related. And, in my view, one of the marks of the success of an analysis is the possibility for us plausibly to juxtapose and compare what to begin with can have appeared utterly incomparable.

Knowing Aristotle's mode of thought, therefore his fundamental purpose in making his system, we assuredly can account (if only after the fact) for his topical program in general and the particular relevance of politics within that program: his uses of politics. Can we identify, within the method of the Mishnah's sages, an equivalently fundamental method or mode of thought? To answer that question, we turn from generalities about myth to the concrete cases at hand. When the framers of the Mishnah speak, it is only in and through detail. But if, as I maintain, their statement is systematic and forms a system, then how they treat any detail of any substance should indicate how they think about all details, and from that indication we should be able to generalize about the methods and modes of thought at hand. And once we can describe how the system-builders think, we can identify what is the generative tension and critical concern of the system as a whole, a tension worked out, a concern expressed, also in the realm of politics.

For that purpose we move as we did before, from the myth of power to the institutions thereof. When the Mishnah's sages address the description of institutions, what is it that they want to know about them? That is to say, given a topic, they will have a particular program of inquiry they propose to follow. They will want to find out, from a scarcely limited corpus of facts, the rule they seek or invent answers to one set of questions rather than to some other. A particular aspect of the facts will attract their interest, which I call a generative problematic, that is to say, that trait of a topic that generates the problems the system-builders identify and propose to solve. In the case at hand, we turn to the two most consequential matters, the political structures and the political sanctions which, together, constitute the formation of coercive power that defines any politics.

And that inquiry draws us to two issues: the relationship between king and high priest, the catalogue of judicially inflicted penalties. These are utterly unrelated, but they yield a single mode and method of thought and produce results that fall within a single classification. Specifically, they compare and contrast and, therefore, hierarchize. In the matter of institutions, exemplified by the treatment of the king and the high priest, we find silence about questions that engage us, for example, the authority and role of each in the administration of the everyday affairs of particular localities, the way in which people leave and enter office, and the like. But what we are told in exquisite detail concerns the relative position of the high priest and the king, with the main point that the king stands higher in the hierarchy of power and authority than the high priest. The Mishnah's framers want to accomplish the hierarchization of these two important loci of power, so they compare the king to the high priest and in detail make explicit the standing imputed to each. By consequence, as I said, the high priest is shown to be a subordinate figure, the king an autocephalous authority. Then the generative issue concerns hierarchization, which is to say, comparison and contrast of species of the same genus. The two heads of state are alike but different, and the king is the superior figure. The high priest and the king form a single genus, but two distinct species, and the variations between the species form a single set of taxonomic indicators. The one is like the other in these ways, unlike the other in those ways. The passage begins as follows:

2:1-2
1. A   A high priest (1) judges, and [others] judge him;
   B.   (2) gives testimony, and [others] give testimony about him;
   C.   (3) performs the rite of removing the shoe with his wife....
                                              M. Sanhedrin

2. A   (1) The king does not judge, and [others] do not judge him;
   B.   (2) does not give testimony, and [others] do not give testimony about him;
   C.   (3) does not perform the rite of removing the shoe, and others do not perform the rite of removing the shoe with his wife....

The formal traits of the matched sets make immediately clear the mode of thought at hand, which, in context, is hierarchization through the comparison and contrast of the traits of office-holders. We know the proper place of each because we can identify the rules that govern them both, and, further, we know the meaning of the application of a rule to one species but not to another of the same genus. The comparison is the point, and we learn that the king enjoys a higher standing than the high priest. Then what the system-builders want to know about the king and the high priest is the answer to a hierarchical question. That explains why they adduce in evidence the facts that they have chosen, rather than other facts that can have been discovered or made up in answer to a generative problematic of another character entirely.

The same point of interest animates discussion on the modes of inflicting the death penalty. The generative problematic comes to expression in the initial introduction of the vast treatment of that topic, as we remember:

7:1
   A.   Four modes of execution were given over to the court [in order of severity]:
   B.   (1) stoning, (2) burning, (3) decapitation, and (4) strangulation.

C.   R Simeon says, "(2) Burning, (1) stoning, (4) strangulation, and (3) decapitation."

Mishnah-tractate Sanhedrin

At stake in the dispute is the severity of suffering imposed by each mode of execution. Simeon's order, C, differs from that of B, in the degradation and suffering inflicted on the felon. Here, again, we find at stake the matter of hierarchization of a genus and its species. These two examples suffice to make the simple point that, time and again, the framers of the Mishnah address to political topics the generative problematic defined by hierarchization. A sustained inquiry into the generative logic of the Mishnah demonstrates precisely the same fact. The Mishnah's authorship's system is a work that in its treatment of facts not only orders things, but also conducts its entire process of thought through modes of establishing connections and drawing conclusions that by definition hierarchize.[16]

That indicative trait of the system as a whole explains why, as a matter of fact, their entire politics is a politics of hierarchization. At stake are answers to these questions: how to determine the correct ordering of society by appeal to who is on top, who underneath? who comes first, who comes next? the right arrangements, the proper and correct positions, for all persons and all things? Just as Aristotle everywhere seeks the answer to one question, systematically worked out in diverse areas, so too do the sages of Judaism. Aristotle consistently wishes to know what is good for humanity, a question he answers by appealing to the natural traits of persons and things to answer the question, so the philosophers of the Mishnah want to answer their question. It is a question that they answer, also, by appealing to the natural traits of persons and things, traits that they work through inductively in question of the pertinent rule or generalization. Aristotle, we recall, appeals to the capacity of humanity to speak, and this forthwith forms a fact of nature that dictates a trait of politics as well:

> Nature...does nothing without some purpose, and for the purpose of making man a political animal, she has endowed him alone among the animals with the power of reasoned speech. Speech is something

---

[16]In point of fact, the entire mode of thought of the Mishnah is that of *Listenwissenschaft*, the science of list-making. I have dwelt on that point elsewhere, and it would carry us far afield to review it. But the upshot is the same, since list-making by definition is hierarchizing, a list constituting an ordering, either of the items on that one list, or of the contents of several lists that are juxtaposed. See my *Formation of the Jewish Intellect. Making Connections and Drawing Conclusions in the Traditional System of Judaism* (Atlanta: Scholars Press for Brown Judaic Studies, 1988).

different from voice...speech serves to indicate what is useful and
what is harmful, and so also what is just and what is unjust.

The same mode of thought – appeal to the traits of things in search of
generalization – accounts for the hierarchical positions assigned to king
and high priest. So we juxtapose the sentences of Aristotle beginning,
"Nature...does nothing" with those of the Mishnah that declare, *"A
high priest judges and others judge him, the king does not judge, and
others do not judge him."* Aristotle's thinking about the political
implications of the natural trait of humanity to be able to speak forms
the counterpart to the Mishnah's authorship's thinking about the
comparison of the king and the high priest. Incongruous? Only if we do
not grasp the systems and what is at stake in them. The Mishnah's
sages dealt with politics because they wished to address fundamental
issues of power, and they imposed upon politics the generative
problematic of hierarchization, because that defined their mode and
method of thought. What they wanted to find out, in the description of
the social order, was the right ordering of things, and what they
managed, then, to say, through politics in particular, was that God
disposes of the affects of human freedom.

That is not to suggest that all Israelites were conceived to be equal
and to stand in the same relationship, within the grid of sanctification,
to Heaven. The contrary is the case. A system of hierarchization by
definition concerns itself with the opposite of the equalization of
relationships; it proposes to show how persons (things, places,
conditions as to cultic cleanness – just about anything!) are not equal.
But in the politics at hand, the upshot of hierarchization is the
opposite: diverse castes are unequal, but all male Israelites may
overcome the hierarchical structure imposed by caste. This they do by
entering the category of sage. The sage, after all, truly possesses and
manipulates power, for power comes from God, and the sage is the
master of the message of Heaven.

The modes of thought in hand, let us conclude with a reprise of the
main conceptions on which this politics of Judaism rests. The framers of
religious systems that concern themselves with the structure and order
of society answer urgent questions set for them in the life of society, in
particular questions of economics, philosophy, and politics. To these
issues of the social order, governing the material and intellectual
foundations of the social entity and the proper administration, through
sanctions, of its collective life, they respond with what are to them
self-evidently valid answers. The religious system then comprises
identification of the urgent question and the composition, out of accounts
of the ethics, ethos, and politics dictated (commonly by Heaven) of

final solutions to that critical problem. The Judaism provides one striking example of how people in writing set forth the ethos and ethics that all together comprise a Judaism: a cogent answer to an urgent question. Since in this Judaism we deal with a social entity that in the minds of its inventors also constitutes a political entity in particular, we here consider how in their imagination intellectuals proposed to sort out issues of legitimate violence. For the political entity, "Israel," in this Judaism exercises the form of coercion that consists of the power to tell people what to do and then to make them do it.

In describing, analyzing, and interpreting the politics of Judaism we have dealt with high abstractions. But we cannot permit matters to conclude with so theological a judgment of what is at stake. For, remembering the words of M. I. Finley that stand at the head of this chapter, we have to ask how the politics of Judaism sorted out "the material relations among the citizens or classes of citizens as much as those more commonly noticed between the state and the citizens." The answer is that this politics did not sort out the material relations among citizens or classes of citizens. This is a politics that appealed to indicators of an other-than-material order when it classified persons, social entities, indeed all living things, within an order and a hierarchy. Independent variables, in the imagination of the system-builders, derived from other considerations than the control of the basic means of production. Perhaps, it would be more to the point to say, the system-builders thought that the systemically interesting means of production were not those that produced material things. What mattered was holiness, and how holiness ("the holy" or "the sacred") was defined would then indicate who produced it, that is, who sanctified whom, and how.

So the systemic issues of hierarchization dealt with the ordering of different things on the basis of different traits from those things that are signified by the indicators of material productivity, and that explains why, if Marxists can identify with their views the politics of Aristotle, they cannot similarly appropriate the politics of Judaism. Only in that light can we take into account an economics that utterly ignores most of the actual economy[17] and a politics that treats as null

---

[17]I point this out in my *Economics of Judaism*. The economics scarcely encompasses the half of the population comprised by women, the classes of craftsmen, artisans, those comparable to what we should call the free professions, traders, merchants, other entrepreneurs – pretty much everybody but the householder defined as landholder, hence, farmer. And while it was a subsistence economy, not everybody was a subsistence farmer.

such obviously puissant classes as are comprised of householders. Now we see the full meaning of the simple fact that sages ignored, when treating politics, what proved the critical and central component of their thought when treating economics. When sages in the Mishnah set forth a politics, they concerned themselves not with material relations at all, but with power relationships, and these, they conceived, flowed not from the relationships among classes of citizens but between all Israelites and God. And yet, as I have shown, their conception of power fully conforms with the meaning of power imputed by the most secular of systems, whether Aristotle's or Weber's! So the distinctions are between like entities, and the distinctions signal vast differences.

The Mishnah's system-builders in intellect have composed a world at rest, perfect and complete, made holy because it is complete and perfect. In mythic terms the Mishnah confronts the fall from Eden with Eden: the world on the eve of the Sabbath of Creation: "Thus the heavens and the earth were finished and all the host of them. And on the seventh day God finished his work which he had done, and he rested on the seventh day from all his work which he had done. So God blessed the seventh day and hallowed it, because on it God rested from all his work which he had done in creation" (Gen. 2:1-3). It is an economy embedded on a social system awaiting the seventh day: the divine act of sanctification which, as at the creation of the world, would set the seal of holy rest upon an again-complete creation, just as in the beginning. There is no place for action and actors when what is besought is no action whatsoever, but only perfection, which is unchanging. There is room only for a description of how things are: the present tense, the sequence of completed statements and static problems. All the action lies within, in how these statements are made. Once they come to full expression, with nothing left to say, there also is nothing left to do, no need for actors, whether the political entities comprising king, scribes, priests, or the economic entities comprising householders.

The Mishnah's principal message expressed through the categorical media of economics and politics alike, the message that makes the Judaism of this document and of its social components distinctive and cogent, is that man[18] is at the center of creation, the head of all creatures upon earth, corresponding to God in Heaven, in whose image man is made. Who this man is – whether householder in economics, whether priest, king, or sage in politics – shifts from topic to

---

[18]Woman is subordinate and dependent. Man is the norm and the normal. That is why I can say only "man," rather than, in this context, "the human being."

topic, but the priority of the human (male's) will and attitude in the disposition of important questions everywhere forms the premise of discourse. The way in which the Mishnah makes this simple and fundamental statement is to impute power to man to inaugurate and initiate those corresponding processes, sanctification and uncleanness, which play so critical a role in the Mishnah's account of reality. The will of man, expressed through the deed of man, is the active power in the world. Will and deed constitute those actors of creation which work upon neutral realms, subject to either sanctification or uncleanness: the Temple and table, the field and family, the altar and hearth, woman, time, space, transactions in the material world and in the world above as well. An object, a substance, a transaction, even a phrase or a sentence is inert but may be made holy, when the interplay of the will and deed of man arouses or generates its potential to be sanctified. Each may be treated as ordinary or (where relevant) made unclean by the neglect of the will and inattentive act of man.

Take the probative case of how uncleanness and cleanness work: not systemically inert or neutral, but systemically indicative. The entire system of uncleanness and holiness awaits the intervention of man, which imparts the capacity to become unclean upon what was formerly inert, or which removes the capacity to impart cleanness from what was formerly in its natural and puissant condition. So too in the other ranges of reality, man is at the center on earth, just as is God in Heaven. Man is counterpart and partner and creation, in that, like God he has power over the status and condition of creation, putting everything in its proper place, calling everything by its rightful name. So, stated briefly, the question taken up by the Mishnah and answered by Judaism is, What can a man do? And the answer laid down by the Mishnah is, Man, through will and deed, is master of this world, the measure of all things. Since when the Mishnah thinks of man, it means the Israelite, who is the subject and actor of its system, the statement is clear. This man is Israel, who can do what he wills. In the aftermath of the two wars, the message of the Mishnah cannot have proved more pertinent.

To conclude: the politics of Judaism accordingly began in the imagination of a generation of intellectuals who in the aftermath of the destruction of the Jerusalem government and Temple in 70 and the defeat of a war three generations later in 132-135 had witnessed the end of the political system and structure that the Jews had known for the preceding millennium. Initially set forth in the Mishnah, a second-century philosophical treatise in the form of a law code, the political theory of Judaism laid out political institutions and described how they should work. In that way, these intellectuals, with no documented access to power of any kind and certainly unable to coerce many people to do very much, sorted out issues of power. They took account, in mind at least, of the issues of legitimate coercion within Israel,[19] the holy people, seen then to form not merely a voluntary association such as a community formed around a cult.

Their Judaism encompassed a politics because through politics they found it possible to express their systemic message, one concerning putting everything in its proper place and order. That systemic message explains also why their system's social entity, that is, their Israel, formed a political entity as well. Their "Israel" was supposedly able to govern in its holy land through the exercise of coercive power and not merely voluntary community that persuaded compliance. The setting was an age of endings and consequently beginnings. Everyone knew what was now behind. Within the half-century before the time of the authorship of the document, the Temple of Jerusalem had been destroyed, together with the political structures based upon it, and a major war meant to recover the city and reinstitute an autonomous, even independent, Jewish state, had been lost. But no one could anticipate what would now happen.

Whatever politics had been before time now had no call upon the future, unless the coming generations restored the now-lost structure and system. But that is not what the founders did. They made up a system for which, in concrete, historical time, no counterpart had actually existed in the world and age of which sages had first-hand knowledge. Indeed, whatever political facts deriving from Israel times past – or from Roman practice in their own day, for that matter – the authorship had in hand were drastically reworked. All received information as much as fabricated conceptions served equally to form the essentially fresh and free-standing structure and system that sages made up. From the mid-second-century to the end of that same century, the work of rethinking the politics of Judaism went forward. And, therefore, embedded within the religious system represented by the Mishnah and correlative and successive writings was set forth a politics that would define the reference point of Judaism from that time to the present. But that does not mean the politics of Judaism in its initial statement ever attained realization in the structure of actual institutions and in the system of a working government.

The system of the initial Judaism, while influential for nearly two millennia, never actually dictated how people would do things at all. By the time the systemic document made its appearance a new politics had gotten under way, one that accorded to holy Israel in the holy

---

[19]The power exercised by gentiles, e.g., the Roman government, never entered the picture since it was not a legitimate politics at all.

land, that is, Jews in Palestine, limited rights of self-government, mainly focused upon matters of no interest to the provincial authorities, e.g., issues of personal status, transactions of petty value, ritual and cultic questions that meant nothing to anybody who mattered.[20] But that new politics, with its jurisdiction over things of no account and its access to power of no material weight, in no way corresponded to the formidable conceptions of legitimate violence, exercised through enduring institutions, a well-organized bureaucracy, appealing to a sustaining political myth, such as are set forth here. Nor in the realities of Jews' limited self-administration in the third and fourth centuries, down to ca. 400, do we find actual examples of the workings of the passion, responsibility, and proportion and balance of a concrete system of political life, such as the document's authorship has made up for itself. But the one trait that would characterize all subsequent systems is the one dictated by the initial system. Politics would require the working out of issues of hierarchization, and sages would dictate the composition and construction of Israel's social order.

---

[20]The second politics of Judaism, the one portrayed in the Talmud of the Land of Israel and associated writings, therefore requires systematic description in terms of itself and its categories, so too what I conceive to be the third politics of Judaism, the one set forth in the Talmud of Babylonia and its companions.

Part Three

THE MESSAGE AND THE METHOD: MEANING THROUGH CONNOTATIVE RELATIONSHIP

7

The Philosophical Study of the Philosophy of Judaism: Appealing to Kadushin's Method

Among the dogmas of the past generation of scholarship on ancient Judaism, pride of place goes to the position that the sages in no way drew upon Greek philosophy. The foundation of that position appears firm, since, as is commonplace in accounts of the subject, among the tens of thousands of Greek words in those documents, we do not find in the Mishnah and related writings a single Greek philosophical term.[1] That argument from silence defines the evidence as wholly lexical. If we can find no use of Greek philosophical terminology, we must conclude that the sages of Judaism in no way derived their philosophical method, let alone their specific ideas, from Greek philosophical tradition.

But studies of mine on the economics of the Judaism of the Mishnah[2] yield a different result entirely. What I found was a point by point congruence between Aristotle's economics and the economics of the Mishnah. When, moreover, I moved on to the politics of the Mishnah,[3] the comparison between the political economy of Aristotle and the political economy of the Mishnah proved apt and suggestive. Not only so, but among all the Judaisms of late antiquity only that commencing with the Mishnah set forth a systematic picture of economics and

---

[1]For a broader critique of the past generation of scholars in this area, see my "When Intellectual Paradigms Shift: Does the End of the Old Mark the Beginning of the New?" *History and Theory* 1988, 27:241-260.

[2]*The Economics of Judaism. The Initial System* (Chicago: University of Chicago Press, 1989).

[3]*The Politics of Judaism. The First Structure and System* (in press).

politics – a political economy – at all, and no Christianity prior to Augustine even addressed the philosophical program of politics, nor, as to economics, is their a Christian economics before the high middle ages.

The fact that in the Mishnah we find thinkers who reach precisely the same conclusions as does Aristotle on economics, and conclusions entirely comparable to those of Aristotle on politics calls into doubt the present consensus concerning the isolation of the Judaic sages from Greek philosophy. It further leads us to wonder how it came about that arguments of a narrowly lexical character should have found a paramount hearing. In order to show what has gone wrong, I have therefore to address the fallacy of the lexical classification in the study of the system of Judaism as represented by the Mishnah. What we shall see is a profound misunderstanding – a misconstruction, really – of the modes of thought of the Mishnah. And this will show us, also, that Kadushin rightly showed the way for the study of the philosophical and theological ideas, the system and structure, of the Mishnah and other rabbinic documents, in his insistence that specific words are the wrong point of entry. First, let me explain how the Mishnah carries on its discourse. Then we shall very briefly consider how the method of Kadushin accords with that mode of discourse. And finally, I shall give a striking example of the wrong method of philosophical analysis, deriving from a misunderstanding of the Mishnah's modes of thought and philosophical goals, and how the philological method, in its lexicographical mode, has misled people as it has.

I. The Mishnah's Philosophical Character

On the surface the Mishnah, ca. A.D. 200, a principal holy book of Judaism, is a compilation of rules. But these rules yield regulations on a program of a distinctively and particularly philosophical character, so that the Mishnah in fact is a philosophical writing. Philosophy by its nature generalizes, seeking the one thing that many things demonstrate, the rule that explains diverse data. It appeals, therefore, by its nature not to a philological, let alone a lexical, mode of discourse. Seeking philosophical conceptions by word studies misconstrues the nature of philosophical method. And that is very much the case with the Mishnah, which manages to say one thing in a great many ways, and that thing, as a matter of fact, is philosophical in its character. True, the Mishnah's is a philosophy in an odd and peculiar idiom to be sure. But the document is a work of systematic thought on a sustaining program of issues that, in the Mishnah's authorship's time and place, other philosophers addressed and that people in general recognized as philosophical. The program was one of hierarchical classification: taxonomy, rules of comparison and contrast, generalizations concerning the relationship of species to genus (the like) and of species to species (the unlike), the appeal to data of a remarkably particular character to define the commanding rules of taxonomy. The rules of classification and generalization, the issues of mixtures, the resolution of doubts, the relationship of the actual to the potential (chicken, egg), the role of attitude or intention in the assessment of an action and its consequences (a subset of the foregoing), and the like – these abstract issues of general intelligibility turn out to form the intellectual program of considerable portions of the Mishnah as well. When philosophers practiced philosophy, these are some of the things that concerned them.

My intent when I speak of philosophy, therefore, is very specific. In claiming philosophical status for much of the Mishnah's discourse (approximately two-thirds, reckoned by the number of tractates) I mean more than that there was a rather general philosophy expressed through or by the law, that is, "philosophy of law." I mean, further, something more particular than that the intellects represented here thought in a manner philosophers respected, e.g., in accord with rules of order and intelligibility. I mean, very concretely, that, in the medium and idiom of rules, the authorship of the Mishnah worked out positions on matters of distinctively philosophical interest. They were not lawyers who had a general philosophy, e.g, of society and the social order. They were *philosophers* who happened also to produce law. The bulk (as I said, about two-thirds of the tractates of the document) of their writing, though by no means all of it, is philosophy in the form of law. The Mishnah's program concerns topics, e.g., potentiality and actuality, intention and action, as well as rules of philosophical thought, e.g., the correct manner of classification, that is, assessing mixtures on the one side and hierarchization on the other, or the proper rules governing resolutions of matters of doubt. These rules of thought are specific to philosophy in that they guide inquiry of a very particular order and into a very distinctive set of questions. Once again, my claim is clearly that we deal with discourse of a peculiarly philosophical order, if in an idiom otherwise alien to philosophy as it was carried on in the age and place under study (and in any other age known to me).

Let me spell matters out. The criterion for whether or not a tractate, or the Mishnah as a whole, is philosophical may be spelled out in this way:

1. are issues "generalizable," that is to say, subject to generalization and so exemplary, with principles pertinent to a variety of other cases? In that case we can move from cases to principles encompassing a variety of cases.

2. And, second, are the principles essentially philosophical ones or are they merely ad hoc or legal ones, lacking any profound philosophical character? Here too the issue is defined as exemplarity or particularity, with the added consideration that what must be exemplified is a principle applicable in wholly abstract, not merely concrete and practical, settings.

3. Is the tractate possible, as we now know it, if elements displaying its character as a philosophical discourse are omitted? That is not a question only of the extent to which philosophical principles serve to impart their character on discourse. The issue is not solely or even mainly settled by appeal to the facts of quantity. Rather, it concerns the basic structure and dynamic of a tractate.

A simple example suffices, drawn from my *The Philosophical Mishnah: The Initial Probe.* The potential modes of addressing the subject matter of Uqsin, Besah, Qiddushin, Orlah, and Meilah are surely without limit. There are many varieties of questions one can bring to those topics. But the tractates as we now have them, covering those topics, cannot have been composed without the prevailing concern for the issues of classification and mixtures, potentialities, intentionality. In other words, there can be no Uqsin, Besah, Qiddushin, Orlah, or Meilah without a fundamentally philosophical program of inquiry into the subject matter of those tractates. Not only so, but, in the case of Meilah at least, the philosophy is worked out in sequence and logical order dictated by the character of the philosophical theorems that are laid out.

Issues that we regard as philosophical meet two criteria. First, they are principles that can apply to a considerable range of specific topics. Second, they are subject to generalization ("generalizable") even beyond the limits of the law, for instance, in matters of metaphysics or physics (as with mixtures and connection), in matters of ethics (as with intentionality), in matters of the fundaments of philosophical inquiry, (as with the interplay of the potential and the actual, which meant so much to Aristotle but not very much to the philosophers of the Mishnah). The distinction is clear when we realize that there are modes of thought that serve both philosophy and other areas of thought altogether; these modes of thought are methods. There are, then, topics, that is, principles of a broad and encompassing character, and these form the program of thought of philosophy, or of theology, or of the regulation of society we know as law, and the like.

To reiterate: the Mishnah's principal philosophical program deals with classification of things: identifying the correct taxic indicators, defining the logical taxa, forming the hierarchical classifications. Its problematic, brought to bear upon one subject after another, will require us to set into relationship several discrete taxic systems and then to sort out the consequent confusions or mixtures. The Mishnah's treatment of any given topic will often, though not always, draw attention to the classification of the data of that problem, the sorting out of sets of data that are formed by discrete taxic indicators, and the resolution of issues of mixture, confusion, or doubt (sometimes, though not always, concerning facts). That tripartite program describes the unfolding of no fewer than forty tractates.[4]

II. The Philological Fallacy: Lexicographical Philosophy

In this context, we realize, the philosophy of the Mishnah will emerge through the repetition, in discussion of a great many things, of some one thing. The effort to teach the principles of classification will be carried on over a variety of topics; indeed, to do the philosophical work, one must demonstrate through a vast range of subjects that a few principles guide the work of classification. Then, as a matter of methodological definition, it will not be possible to appeal to the usages of a few key-words in defining the philosophical method and philosophical position of the document. Quite to the contrary, key-words by themselves will produce misleading results; they will obscure the relationships that emerge in what is (in theory) an infinity of cases and examples, and they will provide the false sense that if we understand these few words and how they are used, we know the philosophy that those words convey. The very emphasis on generalizability contradicts the philological method in the definition of philosophy: cases exemplify, and so do words.

---

[4]I have shown that fact in my *The Philosophical Mishnah* (Atlanta: Scholars Press for Brown Judaic Studies, 1989) Vols. II-III. *The Tractates' Agenda.* Forty-one of the sixty-one usable tractates (excluding Avot and Eduyyot) conform to that simple pattern. My classification of tractates is philosophical, scriptural, and other. The forty-one philosophical tractates conform to the rule given here. The scriptural tractates are not philosophical but present only a reprise of information in the Written Torah. Seven tractates prove anomalous, being neither philosophical nor scriptural. An example of the first kind of tractate is Terumot or Meilah; of the second, Yoma; of the third, Tamid or Taanit.

I shall illustrate that fact by reference to a recent study, done as a dissertation for me and then substantially revised for publication, on intentionality or the human will. That study takes up an important philosophical issue within the Mishnah. The issue of intention in part forms a subset of the larger question of classification, since, one important task assigned to intentionality under certain circumstances is to determine the classification into which something falls. Another task of intentionality is to express the relationship of the potential to the actual. For attitude or intention remains in the realm of potentiality until a concrete action brings it to realization. Intentionality is also a critical consideration for the classification of things and the assessment of connection and mixture, e.g., the status of a subsidiary part of an object may be determined by the attitude or intention of the owner or craftsman as to its use; if it is necessary for the use of the object, it is connected, and if not, it is not. So this category really flows out of the first two, that is, philosophical taxonomy, on the one side, potentiality and actuality, on the other.

Now when I first observed the place occupied by intentionality in sorting out issues of the potential and the actual, I was troubled to find this category particular to a few specific subjects; it is not so ubiquitous as I had anticipated it would be, and I was not at all certain that we deal with a philosophical principle of broad interest. That observation drew my attention to a more considerable problem, which is how the philosophers of the Mishnah defined and set forth their classifications of things. For I realized that if intentionality in relationship to the considerations of the potential and the actual proved specific to a distinctive subject, then it was not a philosophical category at all. For, by definition, philosophy sets forth principles that apply to all subjects without important variation. Its task is to generalize, and its propositions must be subject to generalization (conducive to "generalizability"). An account of intentionality in the philosophy of the Mishnah restricted to the Mishnah's treatment of one subject or another bears no philosophical interest, since it does not conform to the requirement of generalizability.

I was misled in my initial impressions because I relied on the revised version of the doctoral dissertation of my former student, Howard Eilberg-Schwartz, *The Human Will in Judaism. The Mishnah's Philosophy of Intention* (Atlanta: Scholars Press for Brown Judaic Studies, 1986). Eilberg-Schwartz undertook his analysis through word studies, with special attention to two words, *kavvanah* and *mahshabah*. The former refers (p. 7) to "the intention with which a person performs an action." The latter refers "to the intention an individual formulates before he or she actually begins to act." Now were Eilberg-Schwartz to have proposed an essentially lexical study, his results would, in my judgment, stand firm. And so far as his analyses focus upon the two words in question, he has produced useful hypotheses. But, as he has shown in later work,[5] Eilberg-Schwartz has a tendency enthusiastically to generalize on the basis of only a small sample of evidence, and the sample is, moreover, not always very well drawn.

The reason is that the Mishnah's philosophers make their points not through selections of particular words, which preserve a distinctive meaning in all circumstances and which singularly express that meaning. Quite to the contrary, lexical studies mislead, because the Mishnah's philosophers work out their ideas through the study of the principles of classification, therefore also of relationship. They find it possible to express their ideas in a variety of ways, not through particular word choices, but through diverse cases that, without appeal to given word choices, make a single point. That fact is shown, with reference to the Mishnah's authorship's theory of intention, by the important place of intentionality in the definition of slavery. There we find absolutely fundamental data on the power of intentionality and its taxonomic authority, even while such words as *kavvanah* and *mahshabah* simply do not occur. The theory of intentionality is fully exposed; its power of classification worked out in profoundly nuanced manner; and the key-words Eilberg-Schwartz chose for his dissertation never appear. Here is how Paul V. McC. Flesher expresses the matter:

> This brings us finally to the most important aspect of slavery, a master's capacity to have his bondman perform his wishes. The master accomplishes this feat through his faculty of will – that is, his own capacity to plan his actions in advance and to act in accordance with those plans. In effect, the Mishnah's authorities imagine that the master's will replaces that of the bondman...the bondman constitutes an extension of his master's will.[6]

Flesher's discussion impinges upon the definition of intentionality, making points of fundamental importance to our grasp of the principles of intentionality in the taxic theory and taxonomic structure of the philosophy of the document. He clearly alludes to the definition of

---

[5]See the exchange *Journal of the American Academy of Religion*, Spring 1989, in which I call into question his claim to have discovered a philosophy of language in what seems to me evidences of a literary genre (if that).
[6]Paul Virgil McCracken Flesher, *Oxen, Women, or Citizens? Slaves in the System of the Mishnah* (Atlanta: Scholars Press for Brown Judaic Studies, 1988), pp. 160ff.

mahshabah that we have found in Eilberg-Schwartz's dissertation. But the word does not occur, and, conversely, in his book, the passages critical to Flesher's discussion are not discussed at all. That accounts for Eilberg-Schwartz's missing Flesher's contribution to the discussion of the power of intentionality, which is his definition of what the framers mean by the conception of "will" (p. 162-3):

> The Mishnah's framers base the householder's power of will on his capacity to reason. Reason constitutes the mind's ability to understand information and ideas. A person's will, by contrast, comprises his capacity to use reason to deliberate and to make decisions regarding his future actions. The householder's power of will thus enables him to consider possible courses of action and their ramifications so that he can arrive at a reasoned judgment about what he wants to do.

I look in vain in Eilberg-Schwartz's account of intentionality for discussion of the role of reason in the formation and recognition of affective intentionality. The reason is that Eilberg-Schwartz has relied upon lexical media for the identification of relevant passages, and his account therefore is asymmetrical to the philosophical medium of the Mishnah. That medium of thought, as I said, appeals to the discussion of problems of classification, on the one side, and relationship, on the other, for the full and complete presentation of philosophical principles. And that is a mark of the philosophical mind, which seeks to generalize beyond cases and therefore cannot limit itself, in the end, to the data that are generated by cases, e.g., of a particular order. Once the criterion for a philosophical quotient of a representation of thought is generalizability, then the lexical approach, convenient though it is, falls away as insufficient.[7]

III. Kadushin's Correct Definition

In *Organic Thinking, a Study in Rabbinic Thought* (New York: The Jewish Theological Seminary of America, 1938), Max Kadushin made the move from the philological to the philosophical reading of the rabbinic writings. This he did in his invention of the category, "organic thinking," in which he stressed that through a variety of concrete expressions a given complex came to formulation. The clear implication is that we cannot accomplish the analysis of rabbinic thought by appeal to specific words, word studies, lexical analyses, philology. To

---

[7]That is not to suggest that Eilberg-Schwartz's results are unreliable. For the passages of the Mishnah that he discusses, the results are insightful and interesting. It is to say that his generalizations are, if probable, at this moment insufficient because untested against the full range of evidence.

be sure, Kadushin's definition of what we do instead of philological study of conceptions proved hopelessly confused: "the complex of concepts as a whole enters into the constitution of every concept; and thus every concept is in constant, dynamic relationship with every other concept" (p. vi). That is an invitation to total confusion. But in emphasizing the "organismic" character of rabbinic thought, Kadushin did show that definite concepts or terms interrelate and hence a clear definition of a concept cannot be attained through the study of specific words. Kadushin's error is quite specific:

> There can be no real amalgam of philosophy and religion, no sound philosophy of religion, for the reason that in any philosophical system all the ideas are related to one another in tight logical sequence whereas religious concepts are organismic, non-logical. A religious complex of concepts therefore cannot be made part and parcel of a philosophical system.

If the Mishnah stands for a religious, not only a philosophical system, then Kadushin is wrong. But his basic initiative in distinguishing concepts from words that convey concepts assuredly opens the way toward a more appropriate medium for description, analysis, and interpretation of the ideas that, in a given rabbinic document, form a system and an orderly account of things.

In the second edition of *The Rabbinic Mind* (New York: Blaisdell Publishing, 1965), Kadushin formulated matters more successfully. He insisted that "rabbinic concepts" that are represented by single words or terms in fact are "connotative or suggestive....This is to say that they are not definable and furthermore that they cannot be made parts of a nicely articulated logical system or arranged in a hierarchical order. Nevertheless, despite being simply connotative, these rabbinic terms are genuine concepts, general ideas, although neither scientific nor philosophic concepts, nor yet concepts referring to objects or relations in sensory experience" (p. vii). Here again, it is the negative aspect of his argument that I find useful: words are at best connotative, and, it must follow, the philological method in the study of ideas is misleading. In my language, it contradicts the character of the evidence that is studied.

IV. Demonstrating Kadushin's Methodological Thesis

How to proceed? In order to show the right way to do things, which is Kadushin's insistence on dealing in the inquiry into conceptions with context rather than with specific words, I shall give a brief account of a much larger survey of the place of intentionality in the system of the Mishnah – I claim, in the philosophy of the

Mishnah. I cite part of my survey of the sixty-one tractates of the Mishnah that are subject to analysis. In the portion of the catalogue that follows, I list all pericopes in which the issue of intentionality plays an important role. What we see is that intentionality is in play in numerous examples in which the key-words of *kavvanah* and *mahshabah* simply do not appear, because the generalizations, the philosophical principles, of intentionality or attitude come to expression in a variety of words, and, more to the point, in the setting forth of a vast range of cases. The Mishnah speaks about value concepts without identifying particular words for the expression of those concepts, because the Mishnah is interested in classification. Concepts come to the surface through the portrayal of relationships, and these are, in the nature of things, abstract and amenable to representation in a variety of ways (narrative, for one example, through conundrums, for a second, through the invention of problems requiring us to sort out intersecting and contradictory taxic indicators, for a third, and on and on). The worst way to study a value concept is to light upon a few key-words and see how they are used: the intellectual genus of the philological method in its lexical species.

The catalogue that follows serves only to indicate the fallacy of the philological method when it applies to the issue of the human will. I hasten to add that, even here, I did not identify the passages on the principles of attitude, intentionality, and will that Flesher has discussed, and that fact shows the full dimensions of the analytical work that awaits accomplishment. But here is a list that far transcends the rather limited base selected by Eilberg-Schwartz for his dissertation. Whether a survey will require us to set aside his generalizations is not to be gainsaid. The work of describing, analyzing, and interpreting the human will in Judaism, in the context of the Mishnah, awaits.

1. Abodah Zarah

The principal consideration of M. Abodah Zarah 1:1-5 is not to contribute to the joy of the idolator in the celebration of his rite. That consideration appeals to the concern for attitude and intention, not concrete deed; one cannot assist in the celebration, in however remote a manner. M. Abodah Zarah 3:5 appeals to attitude. If one makes use of an idol's property with the intent of expressing offense, then that act is permitted; if it is to express respect, the act is prohibited. The entire colloquy makes the point that the attitude with which a deed is done defines the character and consequence of the deed. M. 3:6 reverses that point; if the gentile has not treated an object as an idol, then its status is unaffected, and an Israelite may make use of that object, e.g., a mountain.   M. Abodah Zarah 3:7 presents an absolutely standard exercise in systematic classification by appeal to the indicative traits of the object under discussion.   But the traits are imposed through differing attitudes or intentions as to the use of an object.   If a house to begin with was built for purposes of idolatry, it is in one classification; if it is built for a neutral purpose and renovated for that purpose, it is in a different category; and if one's intention, vis-à-vis idolatry, has no effect upon the house, it is in yet a third category.   The same differentiation applies to the *asherah*.   The operative consideration at M. Abodah Zarah 4:3 is attitude.   Israelites may do nothing that may contribute to the support of idolatry, and if the Israelite assumes that what he does makes no contribution to that purpose, the act is permitted.   At M. Abodah Zarah 4:4-6 the gentile has power of intentionality over the idol, the Israelite does not.   Hence when the gentile nullifies the idol, it is deemed null, but if an Israelite does so, his power extends only to an idol that belongs to him himself. Nullification involves deed, not merely an attitude; one must do something to express one's attitude that the thing is null and of no account.   God's actions are aimed at changing attitudes, so M. Abodah Zarah 4:7E-F.

2. Baba Batra

At M. B. B. 1:3, 4, 5 we assume that since the landowner has indicated by his action that he approves the building of the wall and wishes to take advantage of it, he has shown his intention and is required to pay the cost of the wall that he proposes to exploit.   The action now bespeaks the (prior) intention.   The consideration here and through the remainder of Chapter Four and half of Chapter Five (M. 4:1-9 and 5:1-5) is the definition of the intention of a person who has purchased or sold a property.   If one has sold one thing, he sells everything that falls into the classification of that thing, but nothing that does not.   The remainder of the chapter spells out the same matter. At stake then is the definition of the intention of the seller and buyer. The established classifications or definitions of things are assumed to define the intentionality, also, of individual participants in any given transaction.   We do not make provision for idiosyncratic readings of a transaction.   At M. Baba Batra 5:6 we see how we do take account of intentionality in a transaction.   If the conditions of sale turn out to be contrary to what one or the other party has assumed, hence the intentionality, for the transaction, of both parties, the injured party may retract.   If the conditions of sale are precisely as represented, there is no injury to prior intentionality, so neither party may retract.   If the conditions of sale are different from the way in which they were represented but there is no clear advantage or disadvantage, both parties have the right to retract. At issue at M. Baba Batra 6:1-4, 5-7, 8 is the unstated stipulation that a person entered a transaction with a given intention in mind. If one sells produce without saying whether it is for food or seed and the purchaser plants the grain and nothing sprouts, he has no recourse to the merchant, who may claim that his intention was to sell the seed for food, not for planting. There are further unstated stipulations at M. 6:2, 3, 4, 8. In all these cases we impose the prevailing attitude or intentionality upon all transactions. M. Baba Batra 9:6 interprets a person's intentions by appeal to his actions. Since the man left himself a piece of land, his intention was merely to make a valid gift, and this is not a gift in contemplation of death, such that, if the man recovers, we invalidate the gift as based on incorrect premises. Hence, the case illustrates the interesting principle that from what one does, we reconstruct the prior and governing attitude or intentionality. The issue at M. Baba Batra 10:5 is the intent of the one who makes the statement. Yosé sees the intent of the statement to carry out the stipulation, and Judah does not take seriously the statement, seeing it as merely an effort to appease the lender, not to propose to pay again what he already has paid. So here the framers of the law interpret intentionality in reference to statement, not deed, and, as is clear, it is not at all certain that, in such a case, we are prepared to impute to a party who has done nothing at all a clear intent as to what he wishes to do.

3. Baba Mesia

The important point of M. Baba Mesia 3:9 is that when the owner of a bailment expresses his intention as to the handling or disposition of the bailment, then that intention governs the transaction, and for any violation of that intention the bailee is culpable. But then should the intention of the owner of the bailment be observed and the bailment be damaged, the bailee bears no responsibility at all. One's attitude or intention is null when in contradiction with the law of the Torah. That fundamental principle, expressed at M. Baba Mesia 7:11, places a close limitation on the effect of intentionality. A paltry sum is not subject to litigation because it cannot be subject to anyone's prior intentionality; no one would have paid attention to so minor a consideration, so M. Baba Mesia 8:5.

4. Baba Qamma

Judah at M. B. Q. 6:5 maintains that one bears full responsibility for what he has done. Even though he may not have known that there were utensils in the sack of grain and therefore cannot have intended to burn them up, in point of fact he has done exactly that. What he has done defines what he wanted to do. Sages charge the man only for what he has done, but concede that a person has to exercise foresight, F-G. One is responsible for a crime only if one has intentionally committed that crime, for M. B. Q. 10:1 maintains that unwitting beneficiaries of a theft do not have to make restitution. One must avoid dealing with persons who are assumed to have stolen property, D-E. That forms the fine line between intentional theft, for which one is responsible, and unwitting theft via a third party, for which one is not responsible, but which one must avoid where *prima facie* evidence suggests that thievery is an issue. In assessing the transfer of ownership, we take account of the attitude of the original owner of property that has come into someone else's hands, whether legally or by theft. Once the owner has given up hope of retrieving his property, the property falls outside of his possession and is available for the acquisition of another party, so M. B. Q. 10:2. An unspecified stipulation is null; we do not assess the attitude or intentionality of a participant to an action and impute to a person a stipulation that he has not made explicit, so M. B. Q. 10:4. This limits the position of M. B. Q. 10:2: we do at some point assess the attitude of the owner of property, basing our judgment on the probabilities that the owner has given up hope of retrieving what is his. At that point, when we believe the owner's attitude has changed, the status of the object also shifts. At M. B. Q. 10:10 at stake in the division of these remnants is whether or not the householder, that is, the owner, takes account of them and deems them of value. If he is assumed to regard them as valuable, then the craftsman may not keep them. If he is assumed to regard them as null, then the craftsman may take possession of them. This is a replay of the conception of nullification of ownership through an act of will.

5. Berakhot

M. Ber. 2:1 introduces the consideration of attitude or intention in the setting of the recitation of the Shema. If one has had the intention of carrying out one's obligation to recite the Shema when in fact he did recite the Shema, then he has completed the obligation to do so. Otherwise, he has not. If, therefore, one recited the words for some other purpose, that act is null so far as the obligation to recite the Shema is concerned. Accordingly, when assessing whether or not one has carried out his obligation, the principal consideration is that one intend to do so. At stake at M. Ber. 4:4-6, 5:1, is that the Prayer not be a matter of mere habit, and that introduces the consideration of attitude. Carrying out the obligation of the Prayer requires the opposite of doing so with the Shema; the one – the Shema – must be done in an attitude of obligation, the other, in a fresh way, as supplication. Joshua provides for a supplication of an abbreviated order, congruent to the circumstance, so sustaining Eliezer's basic position. The matter of "directing the heart" toward a specific location then places yet another consideration into play when we take up the correct attitude for the Prayer. The lamp and spices, M. Ber. 8:6A-C, have been affected by the purpose of those who have already made use of them. Hence attitude or intention plays a critical role in the classification of things. The issue of M. 8:6D is congruent. We wish to ascertain that the lamp's light has served for the purpose of illumination and for no other purpose; then it falls into the classification of what may serve for the present purpose, which is to recite a blessing over the creation of light. So all things are classified by the attitude of man, who makes use of them.

6. Besah

M. Bes. 1:2 (also M. Bes. 1:5-6) takes up the definition of the inclusionary or exclusionary character of intentionality. The House of Shammai at M. Bes. 1:2 maintain that one's intentionality is general, covering whatever is required for the accomplishment of one's basic purpose. The House of Hillel take an exclusionary view and regard as subject to one's intentionality only the specific action that one has contemplated in advance, not the ancillary actions associated therewith. Note also M. Bes. 1:3. Now the House of Hillel dissociate action from intention, and the House of Shammai regard a concrete action as required in the expression of intentionality. M. Bes. 1:4 underlines this, that the ones that are taken are the ones that were actually designated on the prior day.

M. Bes. 2:3C, D, one's purpose in immersing utensils affects matters. If one has immersed utensils intending to make use of them for one purpose and then decides to use them for some other, the utensils require a second immersion.

M. Bes. 3:2 raises the issue of designation, that is, explicit expression of intention. If one has not explicitly expressed intention concerning a particular item, that item is deemed unavailable for use on the festival day, even though one might in general have wanted that category of item. Hence intention must be specific to the item that is supposed to be affected (here: permitted for use) by the act of intention. This same question is in play at M. Bes. 4:3, where one has not designated the beams in advance of the festival for use on the festival in cooking food. This intervenes between the potentiality for such use and the actuality of using the wood for that purpose. At M. Bes. 4:6, 7,

Eliezer regards as adequately designated for use in advance an object that can serve a variety of purposes; any of these purposes is permitted, even when not signified in advance. M. Bes. 5:7 makes this same point, that there should be a prior act of designation, now in connection with the transport of food. If the owner has in advance of the festival assigned ownership of food to his guests, then they may carry that food home; but if not, they may not do so.

7. Erubin

One may establish residence for purposes of the Sabbath in some place other than the normal abode by making provision for eating a meal at that other place. Doing so allows the person to measure his allotted area for travel not from one's ordinary residence but from that other place; the measure is 2,000 cubits. In order to establish a symbolic place of residence, one has to set out prior to sundown on the Sabbath or festival a symbolic meal, or through a verbal declaration accomplish that same end by a specific statement of one's intention and will. One's action, either through placing the meal or an act of speech, accomplishes the purpose; a mere unstated thought does not. In that sense, the provision of the symbolic meal constitutes a powerful judgment that intention by itself is null. At. M. Erub. 3:5 we deal with stipulations that may be made in forming and expressing one's intention. It is entirely acceptable to stipulate in advance a variety of prior intentions, to be worked out in terms of what actually comes about after the fact.

At stake at M. Erub. 4:1-3 is the role of intentionality. If one has not meant to violate the Sabbath limit but has done so, he is nonetheless bound by what has happened, whether to his advantage or disadvantage. But if one's intention was to save life, then that mitigates the situation. So the role of intention is dual: personal, in which it is null, and in the public interest, deemed a prior and prevailing, if unstated, stipulation.

The role of intentionality is further investigated at M. Erub. 4:4. Someone has settled down on a road not realizing that he is near a town. Meir says that one must have the prior intent to establish his Sabbath residence in a town in order to share the benefit of its Sabbath limit. The man had no such prior intent; he stays where he is. Judah says he may enter the town; intention is no issue, for here we deal with error. M. Erub. 4:5 goes on to someone who fell asleep Friday afternoon and did not realize it had gotten dark. Yohanan b. Nuri has the man establish his Sabbath limit where he slept; intention is not an issue at all. Sages insist on a prior act of intention. M. 4:6 builds on this matter. At M. Erub. 4:7-9, 10+11, we have someone on a journey who comes near the territory of his town. He may designate his Sabbath residence by a mere verbal declaration. He refers to a given place that he knows and calls that his Sabbath residence, even though a distance from the place. A mere verbal declaration of intention, without an associated action (e.g., setting out the symbolic meal) is acceptable. The interesting question, M. Erub. 7:11, is whether one may prepare a meal without a person's knowledge and consent. One authority says that that is the case when the commingling of the domains of courtyards is at stake, for that serves only to benefit all concerned. But if it is a matter of setting a meal out to allow travel in a given direction beyond the limits of a town, then the one involved must give his consent, since in gaining the right to travel in one direction, he loses the right to travel in the other. Intentionality is not required when a person must only benefit; we impute automatic agreement in such a case.

8. Gittin

The writ of divorce must be prepared for a particular case and not drawn from an available stack of blank documents, M. Git. 3:1-1, 3. The intentionality of the scribe must focus upon the particular woman for whom the writ is prepared, and the particular husband who gives the order; it must be for a specific wife among several. The introduction of the issue of intentionality in the preparation of the document makes the action very specific. It insures that the husband's intention is fully set forth and fully carried out, since the marriage itself is formed of an act of concurring wills of the husband and the woman or the man who controls her at the time of betrothal and marriage. The initial stipulation of the husband has stated his intentionality, and that must be followed, as specified at M. 3:5D, "for it is not the wish [of the husband] that his bailment should fall into someone else's hands." The reason that a person who has inadvertently changed the status as to cleanness or tithes of someone's produce is not liable, M. Git. 5:4, is that he has done nothing to change the intrinsic character of the produce. The issue as to punishment is settled by intentionality. If one has deliberately mixed heave-offering into the produce of someone else, he is culpable; if he did so inadvertently, he is not. M. Git. 6:1-3 carry forward the interest in the power of intentionality over the transaction of divorce. The husband's instructions predominate, M. 6:1A-C, since he has set up a condition, which then must be met. When the wife establishes a condition, that condition must be met so long as her husband has not set up a countervailing one. The upshot is that the power of intentionality is worked out, with the husband's taking precedence over the wife's. The issue at M. Git. 6:6, 7:1 involves the assessment of the intention of a person who makes the statement. If we assume that the intention of the man is valid, e.g., he expects to die and does not want his wife to remain linked to a *levir*, then we carry out the intention. If there is reason not to impute to the man such a valid intention, then we do not. The point at E-F is precisely the same. So here again intentionality plays the decisive role in the transaction of divorce. Again we observe that what has been created through an act of will is dissolved through a valid act of will. Just as the husband's intentionality governs the preparation of the writ, so the wife's governs the receipt thereof. What that means is that the wife must know what she is receiving, M. Git. 8:2A-G, and if she does not know that what she is getting is a writ of divorce, the divorce is invalid. The effect of intentionality on the part of the husband must cease with the writ of divorce. The divorce must totally sever the relationship between the man and the woman, with the result that she is no longer subject to his will or attitude. Accordingly, a stipulation in the writ of divorce that governs the woman's freedom of action after the writ has taken effect is null, so. M. Git. 9:1-2.

9. Kelim

Mishnah-tractate Kelim focuses in the main on an assessment of attitude or intention vis-à-vis the use or purpose of objects, and in that sense, its main point of interest is on the impact of intentionality or attitude upon the classification of objects. The tractate deals with the status, as to cultic cleanness, of useful objects, tools, or utensils. Its main point is that when an object has a distinctive character, form, use, or purpose, it is susceptible to uncleanness, so that, if it is in contact with a source of uncleanness, it is deemed cultically unclean. If it is formless, purposeless, or useless, it is insusceptible. Three criteria govern the determination of what is useful or purposeful. First come properties deemed common to all utensils, whatever the material. Second are qualities distinctive to different sorts of materials. Third is the consideration of the complex purposes for which an object is made or used, primary and subsidiary, and the intention of the user is determinative. As is clear, intentionality is not the only issue, but it is a primary one. Chapter Four restates essentially the same conceptions about classifying utensils as unclean or clean by appeal to their function or usefulness. The interesting conception is that an object has an intrinsic purpose. If it serves some purpose but not the one for which it was originally made, it is deemed useless and insusceptible, so M. Kel. 4:1-4. Then the attitude of the original owner or maker of the object affects the definition and character of the object, with the stated result. The issue of M. Kel. 5:1-2 is the point at which an oven is deemed useful. The general rule is that when an object is fully manufactured, then it is susceptible to uncleanness. But in the case of a clay oven, the oven may be used even before it has reached its full dimensions. Hence we want to know when it is useful, even prior to the completion of its processing. On the other end, if one is breaking down the oven, at what point is it completely useless. And, along these same lines, what are the appendages of the oven that are essential for using it, hence connected and part of the object, and which ones are not essential and therefore not connected? The criterion of classification throughout is function, not form: use, measured by a common consensus on the matter. So the recurrent taxonomic principle is usefulness, but that is adapted to the consideration of purpose or intentionality. Here is a fine case in which classification is affected – and effected – by issues of attitude and will.

10. Kilayim

At stake at M. Kil. 2:6-7 (and elsewhere) is not whether we actually are mixing crops, but whether it looks as though we are doing so. This is made explicit at M. Kil. 2:7C, for example: "for it [the point of the angle of the wheat field] looks like the end of his field." So long as each bed can be readily distinguished from another, different kinds may grow in the same field without producing the appearance of violating the law against diverse kinds. So in this matter the law depends upon attitude and not upon actuality. The same considerations are operative through M. Kil. 3:7, e.g., M. 3:4: "It is permitted to plant two rows each of chate melons or gourds, but not only one, since if it is only one, they do not appear to be planted in autonomous fields" (Irvine Mandelbaum, *Kilayim*, p. 8). So too M. Kil. 3:3: "[If] the point of the angle of a field of vegetables entered a field of another [kind of] vegetables, it is permitted [to grow one kind of vegetables in the field of the other kind, for the point of the angle of the vegetable field looks like the end of his field," in line with M. 3:5D: "for whatever the sages prohibited, they [so] decreed only on account of appearances." We proceed, M. Kil. 4:1-7:8 to the issue of sowing crops in a vineyard. This is permitted if within or around a vineyard is an open space of the specified dimensions. If there is ample space between the vines, that space may be used. But if the appearance is such that the vines appeared mixed with grain, then the grain must be uprooted. The basic consideration is that grain or vegetables not create the appearance of confusion in the vineyard. Everything in the long sequence of rules derives from that single concern. The prohibition of mingling fibers, with particular attention to wool and linen, occupies M. Kil. 9:1-10. Scripture's basic rule is amplified with special attention to mixtures, e.g., camel's hair and sheep's wool hackled together. Here we assign the traits of the dominant component of the mix to the entire mixture. Items that resemble wool and linen but are not of wool and linen, or that are not intended to serve as garments, are not subject to the prohibition. The issue of intention is explicitly excluded. Even if one does not intend permanently to use a piece of cloth as a garment, it still may not be used at all if it is a mixture of diverse kinds, and so too at M. 9:2F. So here the consideration of intentionality is excluded; all that matters is the fact.

11. Maaserot

At M. Ma. 1:1, the rule is that only when the householder by an action claims his harvested produce as personal property must the crop be tithed; that is in general when untithed produce is brought from the field into the home. Hence when the farmer, by an act that expresses his attitude, lays claim on the crop, then God responds by demanding his share of that same crop, owing to him as owner of the Land of Israel. In general, therefore, at stake is the interplay of classification and intentionality. God acts and wills in response to human intentions, God's invisible action can be discerned by carefully studying the actions of human beings (Jaffee, p. 5). Jaffee's treatment of this subject shows beyond doubt the variety of ways in which intentionality plays a role in theological thought as well; Eilberg-Schwartz did draw upon Jaffee's ideas, but only in his footnotes, cf. *op. cit.*, pp. 224ff.

12. Makhshirin

Lev. 11:34, 37 provide the basic facts of this tractate, but the generative problematic is unknown to Scripture. It is that the attitude or intentionality of the farmer in seeing water affect his produce dictates whether the produce has been rendered susceptible to uncleanness. Scripture defines the given, that dry food is insusceptible, wet susceptible, to uncleanness. But the Mishnah's premise lies beyond Scripture's imagination. The issue of the tractate is the relationship between attitude and actuality. How do we know whether the farmer has favored the wetting down of his crop? Do we assess attitude on its own, or do we require an action to confirm our surmise as to attitude? These are the centerpieces of thought. The issue then is, do we decide upon the basis of what one has done the character of his prior intention, that is, of what he intended to do? And that issue, as is clear, involves the appeal to intentionality to classify whether or not something has been made unclean through the application of water.

M. Mak. 3:4-5:8 proceed to classify water vis-à-vis diverse purposes, primary and secondary. If water is used for one purpose, will another purpose be taken into account? M. Mak. 3:4 makes the point that water used for one purpose can impart susceptibility in connection with a second, unrelated purpose. At M. 3:5A-F it is not the man's intention to wet down the wheat. But we ignore that consideration if through his action, not meant to accomplish the wetting down of the wheat, the wheat is nonetheless affected by the moisture. The most important point is at M. 3:5G-I. One's actions define one's (prior) intentions or attitude. Therefore we do not care whether or not a person expressed happiness, but only whether he has done something to take account of the event at hand. At M. 4:2 we take the position that the water is located where it is with the approval of the farmer. The point of M. 4:4-5 is that if the man disposes of the water, in the view of one party, he did not object to its original location. In the other view, the man's ultimate disposition of the water indicates that he never wanted it to begin with. In these and numerous other passages, the same few points are laid out. Intention is confirmed by subsequent action. Intention takes effect, without regard to subsequent action. We take account of intention; we do not take account of intention. All of these issues gain power in the setting of classification of substances as unclean or clean.

13. Meilah

This is implicit at M. Meilah 1:1 in the consideration of the inappropriate intention of the officiating priest, but it is not a principal and generative conception for the composition. M. Meilah 4:1 is clear that if one's attitude toward a substance is that the substance is null, then if one utilizes that substance for a private purpose though it is holy, he has not violated the laws of sacrilege. So the attitude of the person is principal in determining whether to invoke the laws of sacrilege. If something is not valued by the person who uses it, then that thing is not subject to sacrilege, even though it is intrinsically holy. Then holiness depends also upon attitude. This is a firm fact in the present pericope. But it is not a principal proposition here.

M. Meilah 5:1 maintains that sacrilege depends upon the one who does it, not upon the thing to which it is done. That is to say, the category of sacrilege is invoked by the attitude of the person responsible for dealing with a given bit of *materia sacra*. If that person derives benefit from the thing, even without doing injury to it, he has committed sacrilege. That is Aqiba's conception, and it makes attitude the governing consideration. Sages reject this view, and therefore consider null the issue of attitude, regarding sacrilege as intrinsic to the *materia sacra*. M. Meilah 5:4 makes the same point.

The same point is made throughout M. Meilah 6:1-4, 5. Sacrilege is an inadvertent action to begin with; it cannot be done with intention.

Misappropriation of *materia sacra* done intentionally is under a different rubric from sacrilege. Now the issue here is whether or not the agent has done what he is told. If he has, then the employer is liable, if not, then he is. The issues then concern doing what one is told.

14. Menahot

The issue is the impact of intentionality upon the designation of a meal-offering for a given purpose. The meal has to be designated for a specific purpose, e.g., as the meal-offering of a sinner, and it must serve for the particular purpose at hand, e.g., the sin that has come to light. In the case that the meal-offering is presented under some other designation, that is, "not for its own name," than the one for which it was set aside, it is a valid offering but does not fulfil the obligation of the sinner. The issue, then, is the impact of intention upon the classification of a substance that has been made holy. The substance retains its sanctification, but does not serve the purpose that was meant for it. M. Menahot 1:1-2 present this conception. M. 1:3-4 go on to the issue of the improper intention on the part of the priest to eat the residue of the meal-offering or to offer up the handful outside of the correct time or place, respectively. If while effecting one of the four principal actions in connection with preparing the meal-offering, which are taking the handful, putting it into a utensil, bringing it to the altar, and offering it up, the priest should form the intention of eating his share or burning the handful outside of the courtyard, the improper intention has classified the meal-offering as invalid. And that is without respect to the actual deeds of the priest. If he has the notion, while doing any one of these four actions, of eating or burning the meal outside the proper time, the offering is rendered refuse. This conception is qualified. That is the rule if what renders the offering permissible for priestly use has been offered properly. If it has not, then there is no consideration of refuse at all. One authority holds that if the improper intention concerning time comes before the improper intention concerning location, we invoke the rule of refuse. In any event we have an otherwise valid offering. But if one has improper intention concerning place, he invalidates the meal-offering before he has given play to his other improper intention, which concerns time and which alone brings into play the rules of refuse. Why, he asks, should we declare an already invalid meal-offering to be refuse at all? The entire chapter therefore works on the interplay of intentionality and classification of meal-offerings.

The issue is the impact of improper intention on the parts of the offering, that is, can improper intentionality render unfit not the entire offering but only an element of it? That is indeed the case at M. Men.

2:1. Just as improper intention in respect to either the blood or the sacrificial parts of an animal suffices to impart the status of refuse to the whole, so improper intention either in regard to frankincense or in respect to the handful of meal-offering imparts the status of refuse to the whole. The components are inseparable, and what invalidates part invalidates whole. Here is a case in which mixture, classification, and intentionality come together in a single exercise. M. 2:5 goes on to the same problem. One authority takes the view that improper intention affecting the handful but not the frankincense or vice versa will affect the handful, so that it is refuse, and extirpation applies. Another takes the view that the frankincense by itself subjected to improper intention is invalid, but the matter is not refuse and is not subject to extirpation. Sages vis-à-vis Meir say that extirpation applies only when the whole of that which renders the offering permitted is made refuse. There are three positions as to the classification of the components of the offering and their interplay. One is that we distinguish the handful of meal-offering from the frankincense, but if improper intention regarding the time of offering up the frankincense applies, the sacrifice is merely invalid. The second is that in that case it is made refuse. The third is that extirpation applies only when the whole of that which renders the offering permissible is made refuse. M. Men. 2:2 goes over the ground of M. 2:1. M. 2:3-4 make the point that improper intention concerning what is primary to an offering affects what is secondary, but improper intention concerning what is secondary to an offering does not affect what is primary. If one has an improper intention concerning the thank-offering, the bread brought within it is deemed refuse. But if one has an improper intention to eat the bread outside of its proper time, the thank-offering is unaffected. M. 3:1 repeats the matter of improper intention with regard to the meal-offering.

15. Miqvaot

At M. Miq. 2:7-9 we ask whether rain collected in empty wine jars on the roof is deemed drawn water. If not, then we may simply break the jars and allow the water to flow into a collection point and form an immersion pool. If one should empty them out, on the other hand, the water falls into the category of drawn water, pure and simple. Joshua takes the position that the rain collected in the jars is rain water; breaking the jars is permissible, and the water will simply flow into the collection point. At stake is whether by leaving the wine jars out in the rain I have deliberately collected the water, in which case it should be regarded as drawn water. So the issue is the effect of intention upon the classification of the water. The same matter occupies most of Chapter Four. If one deliberately collects water in a utensil, that falls into the classification of drawn water and renders an immersion pool of less than requisite volume unfit, so M. 4:1. Then the issue is, what sort of utensil serves such a purpose? M. 4:2, 4, 5 develop this point, which is subsidiary to the conception that intentionality affects the classification of water.

16. Nazir

The role of intentionality in the reading of the language of a Nazirite-vow is addressed at M. Naz. 1:5-7. Here there is no issue as to the assessment of the interplay of intentionality and action, however, since the man's own statement governs. But that is as it should be, since it is what he has said that imposes restrictions upon him. The basic issue is how specific the language must be, and, as is common, some authorities will want extremely concrete and specific language, which is subject to no ambiguity. Introducing the consideration of intentionality here is misleading, since, as a matter of fact, unstated intention plays no role, and consequent action is not at stake. The issue of M. Naz. 5:1-7 concerns vows taken in error. The issue, then, is one of intentionality. Does the mere recitation of the formula suffice, or must one mean what one says? The House of Shammai in the opening pericope maintain that a vow made in error is binding; we do not take account of intentionality in assessing the action – here: the speech – of a person. What one says establishes prior intentionality, as is the case in other actions. The House of Hillel hold that that is not the case. A vow to consecrate something that has been made in error is not binding. But that is the case, M. Naz. 5:4 makes clear, when the prevailing facts are not known at the time of the taking of the vow. If the facts prevailing at the time of the vow should change only later on, then the vow remains valid. There is no issue of treating the vow as null on account of things that happen later on. This issue predominates throughout the chapter.

17. Nedarim

At M. Ned. 9:1-2 we go over the issue of the role of intentionality in the classification of an oath as valid or invalid. One position is that a vow that is made on an assumption that later proves false is invalid. Hence we take account of intentionality as to an indeterminate future. The other is that only the facts prevailing at the time of the vow are assumed to be covered by the intentionality of the person who takes the vow. M. 9:3-4 carry the matter further. One cannot use as a pretext something that happens only after the vow has been made; at the moment of the vow, there were no false assumptions that shape the intentionality of the one who takes the vow. But if some things appear to have taken place later on but in fact were already realized by the time of the vow, that is taken into account. M. 9:5-10 pursue the same issues of the interplay of intentionality and actuality in the classification of vows.

18. Peah

At stake in M. Pe. 1:3 is the issue of the relationship of intentionality to action. Following Roger Brooks's reading, at issue is whether the farmer must designate produce at the rear corner of his field or with his designation may apply to any part of the field. Simeon's position is the interesting side. The farmer must designate the proper amount of grain while actually harvesting the rear corner of his field, even if he already has designated produce at the front or middle (Roger Brooks, *Peah*, p. 46). So the act of designation is null unless accompanied by the correct action that confirms the stated intention. Intentionality by itself has no effect upon the law that specifies precisely where the "corner of the field" portion is set aside. If that is not a farfetched reading, then at stake is the interplay of intentionality and action, governed by the objective requirements of the law.

At stake at M. 1:4-6 is the classification of crops within the category of peah. How does this come about? The answers derive first from taxonomic definition, then from secondary application of the principle implicit in the definition. M. Pe. 1:4-5 classifies the produce that is liable for peah as that which is agricultural and in the Land of Israel. As at M. Ma. 1:1, when the farmer claims the produce as his own and grows food on it, he must pay for using the earth and leave God's portion for the poor. The evaluation by the farmer of the crop as useful and the act of acquiring the crop mark the point at which peah is to be designated, just as at M. Ma. 1:1 and for the reasons specified there. In general, therefore, at stake is the interplay of classification and intentionality. God acts and wills in response to human intentions, God's invisible action can be discerned by carefully studying the actions of human beings (Jaffee, p. 5). This is made explicit at M. Pe. 1:6: "Produce becomes subject to tithing as soon as the farmer processes it, the critical moment when he takes possession of the food" (Brooks, p. 51). Thus: "At any time [after the harvest, the farmer] may designate [produce] as peah, [with the result that the produce he designates] is exempt from [the separation of] tithes, until [the grain pile] is smoothed over [At this point, the produce becomes liable to the separation of tithes.]"

When is a field a field, and when is it two or ten fields? That taxonomic problem of how many are one, or how one is deemed many, is addressed once more at M. Pe. 2:1-8. The principle of division rests upon the farmer's attitude and actions toward a field. If the farmer harvests an area as a single entity, that action indicates his attitude or intentionality in regard to that area and serves to mark it as a field. For each patch of grain the householder reaps separately a peah-share must be designated; the action indicates the intentionality to treat the area as a single field. But natural barriers intervene; rivers or hills also may mark off a fields boundaries, whatever the farmer's action and therefore a priori intentionality or attitude. So in classifying an area of ground as a field, there is an interplay between the givens of the physical traits and the attitude, confirmed by action, of the farmer. M. 2:5-8 provide excellent cases for the application of these operative principles. A farmer might harvest a single field delimited by physical barriers, or he may harvest two fields in one lot (Brooks, p. 53). In both cases we ask: do the physical barriers define matters? Or does the attitude of the farmer confirmed by his action dictate the field's boundary? And a further issue is whether a field produces a single crop. If it does, then a single portion is designated, even if the produce is harvested on a number of different occasions. Brooks: "Because the householder has ignored the boundaries clearly established by the field's physical characteristics, his actions have no effect. A parallel problem has a tract of land planted with different species of a single genus. Here the farmer's actions are decisive, and, consequently, his intentionality enjoys full play. The applied reason involving issues of classification is fully exposed here.

The issue of M. Pe. 5:7ff. is what constitutes forgetting and what defines a sheaf. The point is that if anyone involved in harvesting and binding the grain remembers that a sheaf remains in the field, by definition that sheaf cannot enter the category of the forgotten sheaf (Brooks, p. 87). The utter absence of intentionality on the part of the farmer, his workers, and also the poor, who may not practice deception, defines forgetting. So here we are given a fine exercise in the definition of the opposites, forgetting and intentionality. Forgetting on the part of man is deemed the act of intentionality on the part of God. Chapter Six pursues the issue of the role of human intention in determining which sheaves must be left as forgotten produce (Brooks, p. 101). What is the status of a sheaf that the farmer leaves behind with the clear intention of collecting the sheaf later on? What if the farmer binds an unusually large quantity of produce into a single sheaf or places an ordinary sheaf in a special location? The intention is revealed through such an act and the sheaf does not enter the status of forgotten sheaves.

Or the fact that the farmer has left the sheaves behind is decisive. We cannot be certain that the householder will ever retrieve the sheaf, so the intentionality is defined by the action, with the result that this is classified as forgotten sheaves.

M. Pe. 7:7 asks whether the classification of defective clusters depends upon objective facts or subjective attitudes. The taxonomic question is worked out by our definition of the meaning of "defective," parallel to the sense of the word "forgetting." Is there an objective standard for the shape of a well-formed cluster? In that case, the farmer must give all clusters that do not conform. Then the whole of the vineyard may go to the poor. Eliezer holds that the category of defective cluster applies because of the farmer's evaluation or attitude. If in his view there will be no crop at all, then whatever the condition of the grapeclusters, they cannot be rejected. The farmer cannot anticipate leaving the entire crop to the poor; his intentionality will then be taken into account.

19. Shabbat

M. Shab. 2:5 sets forth through the contrast of two cases the stunning conception that the violation of the Sabbath is a matter of not only action but also intention or attitude. If one carries out an action, it may or may not fall into the classification of Sabbath violation. If one's intent is not for one's own benefit, then the action is not culpable. If it is for one's benefit, e.g., to produce material gain, then the action is culpable. So intentionality forms the indicative point of differentiation. M. Shab. 7:3 goes on to review a taxonomic principle. A person is liable for transporting an object across the boundaries from private to public domain. But there is an intervening principle of taxonomy that tells us whether the action is culpable. If someone transports something that is not held to be of worth or value, that is, an object of no consequence, then transporting the object produces no consequences and does not impose liability. Then at M. 7:4 we have a list of the minimum volume or quantity of various sorts of food stuffs for the transportation of which a person is liable. These are minimum amounts of food for which an animal or a human being will find meaningful use, e.g., a mouthful of food and the like. The upshot is that the attitude or intentionality of a human being is taken into account. But this is not left to subjective considerations, e.g., what an individual person may deem of worth or not of worth. There is a limit as to subjectivity in the objective quantities held to be of value to anyone, if not to a given person. The consideration, then, of what is deemed to be valuable is not left in the hands of the private person. I cannot imagine a more profound statement of that principle of the taxonomic power of intentionality than the one in hand. M. Shab. 10:4 once again introduces the consideration of intentionality. If one intended to violate the law but did not actually do so, he is exempt from punishment. If he intended to transport an object in front of him in the normal way but it slipped around behind him and was carried in an unusual way, he is exempt. If he intended not to violate the law but did so, he is liable. M. 10:5 adds that if one performs a prohibited act of labor for some purpose other than the commission of that act of labor itself, he is exempt from liability. If it is permitted to carry an object and one by the way carries a container for that object, he is not liable.

The interest of the framers of this tractate in defining the correct purpose of things and in identifying the intentionality that has affected things, by appeal to that correct purpose, for use on the Sabbath, comes to the fore at M. Shab. 3:6, a somewhat odd item. The principle here is somewhat more complex than it would appear on the surface. The reason is that the oil has been set aside for use in the lamp. That act of intentionality has established the character of the oil. It cannot then be carried. When the oil drips into the dish, the dish too cannot be carried. The dish formerly was available for use; it now has been prohibited, and so its status has been changed, and that cannot be allowed. If the dish was designated prior to the Sabbath for the particular purpose that it now is made to serve, however, then it is permitted for use in that way. That explains the principle of M. 3:6A. The parallel point concerns an old lamp. It is not used because it is undesirable. It falls into the classification of that which has not been set aside for Sabbath use. The new lamp may be used. So the passage overall works on the principle of the classification of objects – permitted, prohibited for Sabbath use – through the prior act of intentionality. We have to revert to Mishnah-tractate Besah to locate discussions of the interplay of intentionality and classification of so sustained and penetrating a character. What has been designated or classified in advance for use on the Sabbath may be handled, but what has not been so designated may not be handled. Here at M. Shab. 4:2 too therefore the question of an act of intentionality is worked out. A hide is available for use with or without food, since it may be spread out and serve for reclining; it is a utensil the intrinsic purpose of which is to do just that. Wool shearings are purposed for weaving or spinning, acts not done on the Sabbath. They cannot be used on the Sabbath. If they are used to cover a dish and keep it warm, the dish may be removed but not restored. Here again the conception of a prior act of intentionality that classifies an object and endows it with its purpose and hence its distinctive character vis-à-vis the Sabbath is paramount. The issue of intentionality or inadvertence is introduced in Chapter

Eleven in these terms: "This is the general principle: All those who may be liable to sin-offerings in fact are not liable unless at the beginning and the end, their [sin] is done inadvertently. [But] if the beginning of their [sin] is inadvertent and the end is deliberate, [or] the beginning deliberate and the end inadvertent, they are exempt – unless at the beginning and at the end their [sin] is inadvertent."

The issue of M. Shab. 17:1ff. is handling objects within private domain. The main point is that objects not set apart for use on the Sabbath also may not be handled lest they be used, while those that serve a licit purpose may be handled and used. That principle is not expressed but presumed. The first issue, at M. 17:1, concerns appurtenances of an object that may be handled on the Sabbath. These two may be handled. They are deemed integral to the basic utensil, even when detached. The issue then is one of connection, and connection here is established through function. M. 17:2 catalogues objects that may be handled. These may be destined for purposes that in fact are not licit on the Sabbath, but if the objects are to be used for licit purposes, e.g., using a plane to cut a piece of cheese, a chisel to open a cask of dates, then they may be handled. So here the principle of classification – permitted, prohibited, as to handling – derives from intentionality. Even before one has actually used the object for its intended, licit purpose, he may handle the object, so the attitude or intentionality establishes the classification of the object, without reference to a confirmatory deed. M. Shab. 17:5 reverts to the question of the initial purpose for which an object is made. Has the attitude of the maker or initial user imparted to the object its ongoing classification, definition, and character? Or do we allow an object to be reclassified by the intentionality of subsequent users? The anonymous authority holds that if a fragment of a utensil serves any purpose at all, even not for which the utensil has been made, it may be handled; that is to say, it is a perfectly useful object. Judah insists that only if the fragment serves a purpose akin to what it served when it is a whole object may it be handled. Only then, when falling into its initial classification, is the object deemed licit for Sabbath use; otherwise it has not been designated or prepared in advance of the Sabbath for use on the Sabbath and therefore may not be used. M. 17:6 goes on to develop the same point. If a utensil is usable only when joined with an object that normally may not be handled on the Sabbath, the utensil and object may be used when joined, but not when they are separated; this is a refinement. The remainder of the chapter works out analogous problems of thought.

M. Shab. 23:1-5 go over actions of speech. The first point is that one may not conduct a business transaction, e.g., a loan, on the Sabbath. One may request a gift and pay the gift back, but one may not establish those conditions that indicate the presence of a formal business exchange. One may not hire workers on the Sabbath for work to be done afterward or ask someone else to do so or wait at the Sabbath limit to do so. Abba Saul distinguishes between speaking of something one may do on the Sabbath, on which account one may wait at the Sabbath limit, and not speaking of something one may not do on the Sabbath, on which account one may not wait at the Sabbath limit. And that distinction carries in its wake a further one, between something one may not do on the Sabbath but may plan on the Sabbath to do afterward, and something one may not plan or prepare on the Sabbath to do afterward. The example has to do with care of a corpse. The upshot is that expressions of intentionality are governed by the requirements of the Sabbath, and actions that convey a prior intentionality likewise are governed by those requirements. Here is a primary instance of the appeal to intentionality in classifying actions as to permissibility or impermissibility, and not only actions, but also acts of speech.

20. Shebiit

M. Sheb. 3:1-4:1 turns to the problem of cultivating the land during the Seventh Year, with special attention to the difference between actually doing so and appearing to do so. There are acts of labor that will not necessarily benefit the field in the Seventh Year, but which may appear to others to do so. For example, one may store manure in the field. But what if this actually enriches the soil during the Seventh Year? Then doing so is prohibited. So how are we to do the work in such a way that we do not appear to be manuring the field? One brings out three dung heaps per seah of land, each of considerable size; then people will not think that it is to manure the field, the heaps being too few and too scattered, so M. Sheb. 3:2. Along these same lines, one may not appear to clear the field for planting (M. Sheb. 3:5-4:1). One can open a stone quarry, so long as it does not appear that the farmer is clearing the land of stones and so preparing it for cultivation. One who tears down a stone fence in his field may remove only the large stones, to indicate that he is not clearing the land, so M. 3:6-7. Louis Newman (*Shebiit*) states, "The sanctity of the Seventh Year depends in the last analysis upon the actions and will of the people of Israel." From a philosophical perspective, what is important is the power of intentionality (here: will) in solving taxonomic problems, assigning to "the class of forbidden or prohibited actions things that the attitude of the community at large deems to be work associated with the Seventh Year or not." What grows in the Sabbatical Year is classified as holy. God owns the crop. Everyone has a right to an equal share. Individuals may not dispose of crops of the Seventh Year as they do of their own produce. That is the fact that generates the interesting problems of M. Sheb. 8:1-6, 7-11. The problem of M. 8:1-2 addresses interstitial classes of produce, which may serve either animals or human beings. How do we know its classification? The matter depends upon human intentionality. If someone gathered it with the intention of using the produce for both human beings and cattle, it is classified by that intention; if someone gathered it only for use as wood, it is so classified, and so throughout. Here is a classic case in which, in an ambiguous case, it is the human attitude or intentionality that defines matters. These same considerations are expressed in the notion of "ordinary mode of utilization," M. Sheb. 8:2. We assume that the prevailing attitude applies in any individual case. Therefore we do not take account of an individual's asymptomatic attitude or intentionality; we classify by the prevailing attitude. M. 8:3ff. then set forth rules for the disposition of crops within the stated rules. The main point concerns the treatment of crops in a manner different from that characteristic of other years of the sabbatical cycle.

The law of removal of crops in the house at the point at which crops of the same classification cease to grow in the fields presents its set of taxic problems. Specifically, we address the interstitial issues involved in cases in which it is unclear when the law of removal takes effect. These cases derive from a situation in which the entire species of produce may or may not be subject to removal at a single time – just the sort of problem of sorting matters out that the philosophy of classification is meant to solve. Here the solution derives from a variety of taxic indicators. First, as we see, farmers in various regions harvest one crop at different times. So one thing becomes many things and is so classified. Sometimes part of the crop has been removed from the field, while part of the same species is growing in a private courtyard or is not yet ripe. Since part of the crop is not yet harvested, the rule of removal should not take effect. But since the species is not now available to everybody all at once, perhaps the law does apply. The taxic indicator is whether the inability of certain classes of persons to gather and eat produce can affect the point at which the law of removal applies (Newman, p. 179). Or perhaps the law is not invoked until the last of that species disappears, without regard to whether particular classes of persons can or cannot gather it. These are the opposed principles that set forth the problems of M. Sheb. 9:1-6. As Newman says,

The first theory is that man through his actions and capacities determines when the law of removal takes effect. If Israelite farmers harvest a single species of produce in two or more separate lots, each crop is deemed a separate entity. Similarly, the ability of Israelites to harvest and use crops of the Sabbatical Year is decisive. As soon as produce of a given species is no longer available...the householder must remove that same species from the home. Finally, the way in which man stores produce after he has harvested it likewise is probative. If a householder stores several distinct species of produce in a single jar, the whole is treated as a single entity. The principle underlying these rules is that man is the center of his world. Through their actions...farmers and householders order the world in accordance with their wishes....The opposing theory is that the law applies separately to each species of produce, no matter how Israelite farmers may handle them....These rules express the notion that it is God's action, not man's [attitude], which determines the point at which the law takes effect.

21. Terumot

At stake at M. Ter. 1:1-2, 3 is how produce is classified so that part of it falls into the category of heave-offering, that is to say, is sanctified. The Israelite is central to the process of classification, that is, sanctification. So Alan J. Avery-Peck (*Terumot*, p. 3): "The holy heave-offering comes into being only if man properly formulates the intention to sanctify part of his produce and indicates that intention through corresponding words and actions. The centrality of human intention in this process is illustrated by the fact that individuals deemed to have no understanding, e.g., imbeciles and minors, and therefore no power of intention, may not validly designate heave-offering." No produce is intrinsically holy. All depends upon the intentionality, as to classification, of the householder. That accounts for the interest at M. 1:1-2 in an act of classification accomplished through full intentionality of someone with the power of intentionality. The indicative traits of those excluded from the process then bear the generalization. We come to the interplay of action and intentionality, with intentionality ruled out of bounds. M. Ter. 1:8 explains how the act of separation takes place. What is required is negative: there must not be a predetermined and measured quantity of produce. The produce that falls into the classification of holy must be so classified by fortune, that is, by accident and not by intention. So the act of classification must be intentional, but carrying out the act must be left in the hands of God. That forms an important limitation upon the role of intentionality, a distinction between the arena in which my intentionality operates, and the boundaries beyond which my intentionality does not extend. The basic principles of the separation of heave-offering having been set forth – intentionality as a distinction, speciation as a consideration – we come at M. Ter. 2:1-2 to the systematic composition of a grid in which the two sets of principles are joined in a common, complex expression. The established rules are [1] heave-offering may not be separated from one genus of produce on behalf of produce of a different genus; [2] if the householder owns different species within the same genus of produce, heave-offering should be separated from the species which is of the higher quality (Avery-Peck, p. 81). M. 2:1-3 begin the work by specifying that heave-offering may not be separated from produce of one genus on behalf of another now with reference to cultic cleanness. The unclean must be treated in distinction from the clean. If one has done so, the act is valid. But what about deliberately doing so, since the unclean is useless and of less value? M. Ter. 2:2 then invokes the consideration of intentionality. If one intentionally separated unclean for clean, his act is null; if unintentionally, his act is valid. Here, therefore, intentionality joins as a principal criterion for classification. The role of intentionality in the classification of part of the crop as heave-offering is spelled out at M. Ter. 3:5. The farmer must express his will distinctly and clearly, meaning he must say where, in his intentionality, that portion of the crop that is distinguished as heave-offering is located within the larger batch. So the oral declaration is required, not merely a decision reached within one's heart, and that oral designation must be detailed and concrete. Only after the offering has been so designated is part of the batch separated and given to the priest. M. Ter. 4:1-6 complete the presentation of rules on the classification of produce. M. Ter. 4:1 allows for the possibility that an owner may wish to give more than the minimum portion of his crop for heave-offering. The established principles are worked out within this context. The issue of intentionality is introduced, now with reference to the volume of the crop that a farmer wishes to set aside for this purpose. The taxonomic power of intentionality comes into play when it comes to violating the sanctity of heave-offering. If a non-priest has eaten heave-offering, how do we classify the act? If he has done so intentionally, he is subjected to one set of sanctions, and if unintentionally, a different set of sanctions, as specified at M. Ter. 6:1D: the principal and added fifth are restored to the priesthood. The added fifth is a fine through which the non-priest makes atonement for misappropriating the sanctified produce (Avery-Peck, p. 193). The task is to indicate who is liable to pay the principal and added fifth, and what produce may be used for that purpose. While the whole of Chapter Six works on these questions of detail, what generates the questions to begin with is the power of classification deriving from intentionality.

Produce in the status of heave-offering may not be permitted to go to waste. It must be used for the purpose for which it has been designated, that is to say, for the benefit of the priest. So the taxic principle that governs the utilization of produce in the status of heave-offering is the initial purpose for which it is intended, that is to say, the benefit of the priest. The intentionality of the farmer in designating this portion of the crop for the priest governs the disposition of the crop, yet another important way in which intentionality forms a primary taxic indicator in the formation of the rules of this tractate. Chapter Eleven spells the matter out. M. 11:1-3 presents the governing theory: produce in the status of heave-offering must be prepared in the manner customary for unconsecrated produce of the same type. What this means is that the intentionality of the farmer-donor is limited by the prevailing practice or rule, though I do not think that that is a principal consideration here. All portions of the produce that normally are eaten must be available for eating (Avery-Peck, p. 295). If produced is processed in an abnormal way, so that what is usually eaten is pressed for juice, the skin would go to waste; that must not happen. M. 11:4-7 proceeds to produce that normally is not eaten but may be consumed. Such an interstitial category demands attention. How do we resolve the matter? If the priest deems that produce worthy as food, then it is in the consecrated status of heave-offering. What the priest does not deem food is treated as inedible and therefore not in the status of heave-offering. Here intentionality has paramount power of classification. M. 11:8-10 deal with produce of an ambiguous classification. It is unclean and may not be eaten by the priest; or he may not want it as food. But it may be used for some other purpose, e.g., fodder or lamp oil. Since it cannot be used as food, it does not have to be eaten; but it may not be permitted to go to waste.

22. Uqsin

M. Uqs. 2:1: If the merchant wants the hair, it is deemed connected, and if not, it is deemed null. If the one who did the pickling deemed the leaves merely for the sake of ornament, then the leaves are not regarded as part of the plant. Hence the attitude or intentionality of the owner of the produce is taken into account when we assess whether an extrinsic part of the produce is regarded as joined with the main part or is deemed not a component of it at all.

Also M. Uqs. 2:5: If the man began to pull the produce apart, we have no reason to suppose that the process of disconnection will inevitably continue; therefore, only the food actually taken apart is deemed disconnected. Hence we dismiss the potentiality of what one may do, even though one's intention is to do exactly that; we take account only of what one actually has done.

Also M. Uqs. 2:6; Uqs. 2:10: Since we do not take account of whether the roots have penetrated but only can penetrate, both at A and, conversely, also at B (the pot with the hole), the issue here is whether the potential is deemed actual, and it is.

M. Uqs. 3:1: There are things which require preparation by the application of liquid, to be made susceptible to uncleanness, but not intention to be deemed edible, intention but not preparation, neither, both. Also M. Uqs. 3:2, 3, M. 3:9.

M. Uqs. 3:4: Once dill has imparted its flavor, it has carried out that for which it is intended and is no longer susceptible to uncleanness as food. The issue of intentionality remains decisive.

23. Zebahim

The basic consideration that is operative in Chapters One (1:1) through Four (4:6), Chapter Six (6:7) is that the priest must carry out his duties with the correct intentionality. That involves several considerations. First, he must conduct the rite in accord with the owner's intentionality. If the owner has designated ("sanctified") the beast for a given offering, e.g., a sin-offering or a guilt-offering or peace-offering, then that is the rule that must govern. Second and more important, the priest must not form the intention of eating his share of the meat outside of the correct location in which the meat must be eaten, and he must not form the intention of tossing the blood beyond the specified period of time during which the beast's blood must be tossed on the altar. If he should do so, then he has classified the beast as unacceptable, and that is accomplished not through deed but solely through the incorrect intentionality that he has formed for himself. M. 1:1-3 deal with the first of the two considerations of intentionality, that is, preserving the animal within the classification for which the owner has designated it. If the priest slaughters a beast other than for its proper designation, it ordinarily remains valid (with the specified exceptions), even though, as to the owner's personal obligation for this offering (incurred by inadvertent sin, for instance), that must be met with a different beast; the stress here is that the beast must be designated for the particular sin that the owner of the beast has inadvertently carried out. Intentionality then plays a role in classification here in that the priest has done the deed with an improper attitude and that has classified the beast in a manner other than the donor has intended; the priest's intentionality is paramount.

M. Zeb. 2:1 lists ten categories of persons or actions that invalidate a rite. What is important is the contrast drawn to what follows, which is, attitudes that have the same taxonomic power. M. 2:2-5 set forth the issue of intentionality. If a priest slaughters the animal sacrifice intending at the moment of the action later on to toss the blood outside its proper location or to burn the entrails or to eat the flesh outside the correct location, the sacrifice is invalid. That is the rule of M. 2:2. If one does so with the improper intention to toss the blood the next day, to burn the entrails the next day, or to eat the flesh the next day, then the offering is deemed refuse, and one who eats of that meat incurs the penalty of extirpation. M. 2:3 generalizes: if the false intention has to do with the place in which the action is done, then the sacrifice is invalid, and extirpation to begin with does not pertain to it. If it has to do with time, the sacrifice is refuse, and extirpation does pertain. M. 2:3 qualifies by holding that these considerations apply only if what permits the sacrifice to be eaten by the priests or donor has properly to be offered up. It is then, but only then, that the sacrifice comes within the category of being subject to the rule of refuse – that is to say, the consideration of intentionality – and therefore also of extirpation. But if what permits the offering to be eaten is not properly offered, which is to say, if the blood is not properly tossed, at which point sacrificial portions of the sacrifice are burned on the altar and the priest's share of the meat may be eaten by him, then the sacrifice is not subject at all to the rule of refuse; the consideration of attitude or intentionality does not pertain. M. 2:4 gives examples of both cases, first, the proper offering of that which permits the offering to be eaten, then the improper offering of that which permits the offering to be eaten. In the former case we have slaughtering without proper intention, then receiving, conveying, and tossing the blood with improper intention as to time; or improper slaughtering, then proper disposition of the blood; or improper intention in regard to time as regards slaughtering, then receiving, conveying, and tossing the blood. Intentionality plays its role here, since it is a factor in consideration whether that which permits the offering to be eaten has been properly offered. That which permits the offering to be eaten is not properly offered if the act of slaughter took place with the disqualifying intention of eating the meat outside the proper place, and the blood was received, conveyed, and tossed with the intention of eating the meat at the improper time; or if the slaughter was accompanied by improper intention as regards the time of eating, and the blood was received, conveyed, and tossed with improper intention as regards the place of eating the meat, and so forth. M. 2:5 adds that the act of intentionality must pertain to a sizable portion of the meat, an olive's bulk or more. If the intentionality pertains to less than that bulk, it is null. M. 3:1 then proceeds to assess the power of intentionality imputed to people who are not supposed to have a role in the rite at all, or who can carry out one part of the rite but not some other. M. 3:2 completes that matter. M. 3:3-5 deal with improper intention concerning matters that are improperly conceived to begin with, e.g., improper intention to eat at the wrong time things that are not normally eaten at all, or to burn in the wrong place things not usually burned at all; M. 3:6 goes on to the limitations of intentionality. Improper intention concerning something that is not normally done is null. Chapter Four draws to a close the discussion of the role of intentionality in the sacrificial act and process. The discussion both pursues secondary issues and then closes with a powerful generalization. M. 4:1-2 ask, with the sprinkling of which particular drop of blood is the false intention to eat part of the sacrifice outside of its proper time going to invoke the status of refuse for that sacrifice? This is surely a secondary consideration. M. 4:3 lists things that are not subject to the law of refuse at all; to these intentionality does not apply. Whatever is subject to the proper offering of that which renders the offering permissible, e.g., for eating by the priest or for burning on the altar, also is subject to the law of refuse, and whatever is not subject to such a condition is exempt, a familiar consideration. M. 4:4 carries forward the same definition. M. 4:5 introduces the matter of the relationships between liability to refuse and liability to the prohibition of remnant, which is to say, leaving meat over beyond its proper time. That is the action to which invalidating intention involved in refuse is relevant. The consideration of carrying the rite on in a state of uncleanness is here introduced as well. Things which are not liable to refuse are liable to the prohibitions as to remnant and uncleanness, except for the blood. That a variety of taxonomic considerations are in play then is self-evident. M. 4:6, given above, tells us that the intentionality of the officiating priest, not of the donor-owner of the beast, is determinative.

What is now clear, and hardly requires extensive reiteration, is that lexical studies provide only limited data, therefore unreliable conclusions, in the study of the philosophical and theological conceptions of a document such as the Mishnah. The reason is that the character of the Mishnah is violated by the identification of pertinent data solely through word choices. The Mishnah's authorship expresses ideas through its account of relationships, that is to say, within the idiom of hierarchical classification, and it is entirely feasible, on that account, to make the same point through a variety of cases, and, it follows, of word choices. The correct medium for mishnaic speech is abstract symbol, but, having no such symbolic vocabulary at its disposal, the Mishnah's authorship chose the next best thing: picayune cases of such monumental specificity as to require, for intelligible discourse, a process of generalization and abstraction. God lives in the details – therefore not only in the word. The tractates surveyed here show that the concept of intentionality (in Kadushin's term) is present even when the language, *kavvanah* or *mahshabah*, is not used, and that the variety and range of meanings or connotations are considerably broader than we imagine when we take account only of the lexical evidence narrowly construed. What follows is the claim of the philological method that because a word does not occur, therefore an idea is not present, is monumentally irrelevant to the character of the evidence (and, by the way, also wrong). Does it matter?

Part Four

AN ANCIENT JUDAIC MESSAGE

8

Oral Torah: The Message of the Living Sage in the Medium of Tradition

1:1.   Moses received Torah at Sinai and handed it on to Joshua, Joshua to elders, and elders to prophets. And prophets handed it on to the men of the great assembly. They said three things: Be prudent in judgment. Raise up many disciples. Make a fence for the Torah.

1:2.   Simeon the Righteous was one of the last survivors of the great assembly. He would say: On three things does the world stand: On the Torah, and on the Temple service, and on deeds of loving kindness.

1:3.   Antigonus of Sokho received [the Torah] from Simeon the Righteous. He would say: Do not be like servants who serve the master on condition of receiving a reward, but [be] like servants who serve the master not on condition of receiving a reward. And let the fear of Heaven be upon you.

1:4.   Yosé ben Yoezer of Zeredah and Yosé ben Yohanan of Jerusalem received [the Torah] from them. Yosé ben Yoezer says: Let your house be a gathering place for sages. And wallow in the dust of their feet, and drink in their words with gusto.

1:5.   Yosé ben Yohanan of Jerusalem says: Let your house be open wide. And seat the poor at your table ["make the poor members of your household"]. And don't talk too much with women. (He referred to a man's wife, all the more so is the rule to be applied to the wife of one's fellow. In this regard did sages say: So long as a man talks too much with a woman, he brings trouble on himself, wastes time better spent on studying the Torah, and ends up an heir of Gehenna.)

1:6.   Joshua ben Perahyah and Nittai the Arbelite received [the Torah] from them. Joshua ben Perahyah says: Set up a master for

yourself. And get yourself a companion-disciple. And give
everybody the benefit of the doubt.

1:7.   Nittai the Arbelite says: Keep away from a bad neighbor. And
don't get involved with a bad person. And don't give up hope of
retribution.

1:8A.   Judah ben Tabbai and Simeon ben Shetah received [the Torah]
from them.

1:8B   Judah ben Tabbai says: Don't make yourself like one of those
who advocate before judges [while you yourself are judging a
case]. And when the litigants stand before you, regard them as
guilty. But when they leave you, regard them as acquitted (when
they have accepted your judgment).

1:9.   Simeon ben Shetah says: Examine the witnesses with great care.
And watch what you say, lest they learn from what you say how to
lie.

1:10.   Shemaiah and Avtalyon received [the Torah] from them.
Shemaiah says: Love work. Hate authority. Don't get friendly
with the government.

1:11.   Avtalyon says: Sages, watch what you say, lest you become liable
to the punishment of exile, and go into exile to a place of bad
water, and disciples who follow you drink bad water and die, and
the name of Heaven be thereby profaned.

1:12.   Hillel and Shammai received [the Torah] from them. Hillel says:
Be disciples of Aaron, loving peace and pursuing grace, loving
people and drawing them near to the Torah.

1:13A. He would say [in Aramaic]: A name made great is a name
destroyed, and one who does not add, subtracts.

1:13B   And who does not learn is liable to death. And the one who uses
the crown, passes away.

1:14.   He would say: If I am not for myself, who is for me? And when I
am for myself, what am I? And if not now, when?

1:15.   Shammai says: Make your learning of the Torah a fixed
obligation. Say little and do much. Greet everybody cheerfully.

1:16.   Rabban Gamaliel says: Set up a master for yourself. Avoid doubt.
Don't tithe by too much guesswork.

1:17.   Simeon his son says: All my life I grew up among the sages, and I
found nothing better for a person [the body] than silence. And
not the learning is the thing, but the doing. And whoever talks too
much causes sin.

1:18.   Rabban Simeon ben Gamaliel says: On three things does the
world stand: on justice, on truth, and on peace. As it is said,
Execute the judgment of truth and peace in your gates. (Zech.
8:16)

2:1.   Rabbi [Judah the Patriarch] says: What is the straight path which
a person should choose for himself? Whatever is an ornament to
the one who follows it, and an ornament in the view of others. Be

meticulous in a small religious duty as in a large one, for you do not know what sort of reward is coming for any of the various religious duties. And reckon with the loss [required] in carrying out a religious duty against the reward for doing it; and the reward for committing a transgression against the loss for doing it. And keep your eye on three things, so you will not come into the clutches of transgression. Know what is above you. An eye which sees, and an ear which hears, and all your actions are written down in a book.

2:2. Rabban Gamaliel, a son of Rabbi Judah the Patriarch says: Fitting is learning in the Torah along with a craft, for the labor put into the two of them makes one forget sin. And all learning of the Torah which is not joined with labor is destined to be null and causes sin. And all who work with the community – let them work with them [the community] for the sake of Heaven. For the merit of the fathers strengthens them, and the righteousness which they do stands forever. And, as for you, I credit you with a great reward, as if you had done [all the work required by the community].

2:3. Be wary of the government, for they get friendly with a person only for their own convenience. They look like friends when it is to their benefit, but they do not stand by a person when he is in need.

2:4. He would say: Make His wishes into your own wishes, so that He will make your wishes into His wishes. Put aside your wishes on account of His wishes, so that He will put aside the wishes of other people in favor of your wishes. Hillel says: Do not walk out on the community. And do not have confidence in yourself until the day you die. And do not judge your companion until you are in his place. And do not say anything which cannot be heard, for in the end it will be heard. And do not say: When I have time, I shall study, for you may never have time.

2:5. He would say: A coarse person will never fear sin, nor will an *am ha-aretz* [who has not mastered the Torah] ever be pious, nor will a shy person learn, nor will an ignorant person teach, nor will anyone too occupied in business get wise. In a place where there are no individuals, try to be in individual.

2:6. Also, he saw a skull floating on the water and said to it [in Aramaic]: Because you drowned others, they drowned you, and in the end those who drowned you will be drowned.

2:7. He would say: Lots of meat, lots of worms; lots of property, lots of worries; lots of women, lots of witchcraft; lots of slave girls, lots of lust; lots of slave boys, lots of robbery. Lots of the Torah, lots of life; lots of discipleship, lots of wisdom; lots of counsel, lots of understanding; lots of righteousness, lots of peace. [If] one has

gotten a good name, he has gotten it for himself. [If] he has gotten
teachings of the Torah, he has gotten himself life eternal.
                                          The Sayings of the Founders

Here is a fundamental chapter of the Oral Torah: The Sayings of
the Fathers (or, I prefer, the Founders). It certainly will not strike the
reader as something similar to anything in what is called the Jewish
Scripture or Old Testament, and in what Judaism calls the Written
Torah. Yet here, and in a whole library of other writings, are
components of that Oral Torah that God reveals to Moses, our rabbi, at
Sinai.

In Judaism, what the great sages teach is part of the Torah, that is,
falls into the classification of Torah-teaching, as much as what we
find in the Written Torah Christians know as the Old Testament. The
claim of Judaism to speak in the name of Moses at Sinai and to hand on
God's revelation to Israel, the holy people, rests upon the authority
and teaching of these sages. For the Torah is mediated to us Jews
through the midrash-exegesis of the great rabbis, as much as the Old
Testament is mediated to Christian believers through the prism of the
New Testament. The medium for the claim is before us: the chain of
tradition. The message is that the Oral Torah then constitutes a
tradition, and that, further, Judaism is a traditional religion.

But on what basis do these sages' views register as authoritative?
Do they come to us as do the statements in the written part of the
Torah, that is, by authority of God's gift of the Torah to Moses at
Sinai? That is precisely the claim in behalf of the authorities of the
Oral Torah that is set forth in Tractate Avot, the Founders. To see how
these sages put forward their claim to authority, that is to say, the
relationship of what they teach to the revelation of God to Moses at
Sinai, is to understand how and why we rabbis teach Israel, the holy
people, to read Scripture as we Jews do.

Before us in the opening sentence lies the important claim in behalf
of the Oral Torah:

> Moses received Torah at Sinai and handed it on to Joshua, Joshua
> to elders, and elders to prophets. And prophets handed it on to the
> men of the great assembly.

The language that is the key is in the verb, receive, hand on. Moses
received Torah, without the definite article that could be understood to
limit matters to The Torah, the Written Torah. Then is introduced the
critical conception, handed it on. The Hebrew word for hand on is
masar, and from that same set of consonants comes the Hebrew word for
tradition, *masoret*. So the path from Sinai to us is one made up of
people who receive and hand on revelation, and that is, tradition. The

main point then is who are the people who stand in this chain of receiving and handing on.

To understand the way in which tractate Avot explains the Torah, the one whole Torah, oral and written, one has to proceed to the list of names: Simeon the Righteous, Antigonus, then some paired names: two Yosés, Joshua and Nittai, Judah and Simeon, Shemaiah and Avtalion, Hillel and Shammai; finally Gamaliel and Simeon his son. Are these biblical names? Some yes, some no. Do they refer to figures in the Old Testament? Not one of them. Then who are they? To know the answer to that question, Christians need only identify the Gamaliel at hand with the Gamaliel in Luke-Acts, who is generally assumed to be the same figure that is mentioned here, and in Josephus' picture of the life and times of the Pharisees in the first century is none other than Simeon b. Gamaliel. Not only so, but if the reader opens the pages of the Mishnah, the second-century philosophical system in the form of a law code, he or she will find as key authorities Hillel and Shammai and their disciples, called the Houses of Hillel and Shammai, respectively.

The point made by this list of names is very simple, therefore, and it is like the New Testament genealogies for Jesus Christ. Specifically, these figures have received, and now hand on, the Torah that God gave to Moses at Mount Sinai. Then the teachings of these authorities and their disciples, that is, students who have acquired Torah teachings through a process of sustained study and imitation of the master, will be in the classification of Torah revealed to Moses at Sinai.

That sages' teachings stand for the Torah of Moses at Sinai, that is, the oral part of that Torah, emerges in another noteworthy detail. Nothing that is assigned to the sages is in the form of a verse of Scripture together with an interpretation of that verse assigned to one of these latter-day authorities in the tradition of Moses. So in order to receive and hand on Torah from Sinai, a sage does not find himself limited to interpreting a statement of the Written Torah, not at all. A sage teaches what he teaches; that forms part of the Torah of Sinai. Torah is as much the saying of Hillel,

> If I am not for myself, who is for me? And when I am for myself, what am I? And if not now, when?

as it is Scripture's "you shall love your neighbor as yourself." And when, in another source, to Hillel is attributed the saying, "What is hateful to yourself, do not do to your fellow. That is the whole Torah in its entirety, everything else is elaboration, now go forth and learn," that too is Torah. It is Torah in Hillel's formulation of it.

Again, when, as we shall now see, a sage works out with his disciples sayings that turn out, as we see them altogether, to be nothing more than elaborations in concrete terms of the same verse at Lev. 19:18: "You shall love your neighbor as yourself," that too is part of the discourse of the master with the disciples in the here and now. It is not merely valid because the Written Torah is cited. It is valid because the master has taught the disciples, through precept and example, that truth. That suffices to find a place for the teaching in the chain of tradition extending upward to Sinai.

> Rabban Yohanan ben Zakkai received [the Torah] from Hillel and Shammai.
>
> He would say: If you have learned much Torah, do not puff yourself up on that account, for it was for that purpose that you were created.
>
> He had five disciples, and these are they: Rabbi Eliezer ben Hyrcanus, Rabbi Joshua ben Hananiah, Rabbi Yosé the Priest, Rabbi Simeon ben Nethanel, and Rabbi Eleazar ben Arakh.
>
> He said to them: Go and see what is the straight path to which someone should stick.
>
> Rabbi Eliezer says: A generous spirit. Rabbi Joshua says: A good friend. Rabbi Yosé says: A good neighbor. Rabbi Simeon says: Foresight. Rabbi Eleazar says: Good will.
>
> He said to them: I prefer the opinion of Rabbi Eleazar ben Arakh, because in what he says is included everything you say.
>
> He said to them: Go out and see what is the bad road, which someone should avoid. Rabbi Eliezer says: Envy. Rabbi Joshua says: A bad friend. Rabbi Yosé says: A bad neighbor. Rabbi Simeon says: A loan. (All the same is a loan owed to a human being and a loan owed to the Omnipresent, the blessed, as it is said, The wicked borrows and does not pay back, but the righteous person deals graciously and hands over [what is owed].) Ps. 37:21.
>
> Rabbi Eleazar says: Ill will.
>
> He said to them: I prefer the opinion of Rabbi Eleazar ben Arakh, because in what he says is included everything you say.
>
> Tractate Avot 2:8-9

A second look at these sayings shows us we have a sequence of concrete applications of what Christians know as the golden rule. It is framed in terms of reputation, property, attitude. But it comes down to the same thing. So the Oral Torah as represented by Yohanan ben Zakkai joins to Sinai the everyday observations of the great masters and his disciples. It does not suffice only to quote the Written Torah. What people observe in the streets ("Go out and see...") contributes to the Torah. And how the disciples transform everyday affairs into Torah teachings forms the centerpiece of revelation as they experience it –

and also adds the revelation they have received to the tradition that forms the Torah.

Let me then generalize on the theory of the Oral Torah that we have seen expressed in these striking details. Tractate Avot, 250 C.E., represents the authority of the sages cited in Avot as autonomous of Scripture. Those authorities in Avot do not cite verses of Scripture, but what they themselves say does constitute a statement of the Torah. There can be no clearer way of saying that what these authorities present in and of itself falls into the classification of the Torah. Specifically, as we see in the opening chapter of the tractate, the authorship of the tractate lists as its authorities Moses, Joshua, prophets, and onward, in a chain of tradition. What makes the chain a statement of the standing and authority of the Oral Torah's authorities is the compositors' inclusion of the names, within the tradition of Sinai, of authorities of the important books of the Oral Torah, beginning with the Mishnah and encompassing later on the midrash compilations we have already consulted at some length. That fact indicates the whole of their polemic: the teaching of the authorities of the Oral Torah derives from authorities who stand in a direct line to Sinai. Then the Oral Torah enjoys the standing and authority of God's revelation to Moses at Sinai and forms part of the Torah of Sinai. A process of oral formulation and oral transmission through the memories of sages links the Oral Torah and the Written Torah alike to Moses at Sinai.

In this way the founders of Judaism work out that problem of Scripture and tradition familiar also to Roman Catholic and Protestant Christianity. But the particular formulation of the problem is not the same. We shall understand the position of the framers of Avot when we recognize the problem that confronted them. It began with a vast law code, the Mishnah, which, along with the law of Scripture, Judah the Patriarch, whom Rome recognized as the ruler of the ethnic group, the Jews, in the province of Palestine, adopted as the basic law for the government of Israel in the Land of Israel (thus: the Jews of Palestine) in around 200. As soon as the Oral Torah in the form of the Mishnah, the first document of the Oral Torah, made its appearance, the vast labor of explaining its meaning and justifying its authority got under way.

How relate the Written Torah to the Oral Torah, which, people maintained, encompassed this law code, the Mishnah? The Mishnah presented one striking problem in particular. It rarely cited scriptural authority for its rules. Omitting scriptural prooftexts bore the implicit claim to an authority independent of Scripture, and in that striking fact the document set a new course for itself. For from the formation of ancient Israelite Scripture into a holy book in Judaism, in the aftermath of the return to Zion and the creation of the Torah-book in Ezra's time (ca. 450 B.C.) the established canon of revelation (whatever its contents) coming generations routinely set their ideas into relationship with Scripture. This they did by citing prooftexts alongside their own rules. Otherwise, in the setting of Israelite culture, the new writings could find no ready hearing.

Over the six hundred years from the formation in writing of the Torah of "Moses" in the time of Ezra, from ca. 450 B.C., to ca. 200 C.E., four conventional ways to accommodate new writings – new "tradition" – to the established canon of received Scripture had come to the fore.

First and simplest, a writer would sign a famous name to his book, attributing his ideas to Enoch, Adam, Jacob's sons, Jeremiah, Baruch, and any number of others, down to Ezra. But the Mishnah bore no such attribution, e.g., to Moses. Implicitly, to be sure, the statement of Avot 1:1, "Moses received Torah from Sinai" carried the further notion that sayings of people on the list of authorities from Moses to nearly their own day derived from God's revelation at Sinai. But no one made that premise explicit before the time of the Talmud of the Land of Israel of the Land of Israel. We note, in this connection, that the authors of the Gospels took the same view as did the authors of the Mishnah. They too did not sign the names of Old Testament authorities. They explained the origins of Jesus Christ by appeal to genealogy, just as, in tractate Avot, we find an explanation of the origins of the Oral Torah by appeal to genealogy: the genealogy represented by tradition.

Second, an authorship might also imitate the style of biblical Hebrew and so try to creep into the canon by adopting the cloak of Scripture. But the Mishnah's authorship ignores biblical syntax and style. And the Gospel's authors of course did not even try.

Third, an author would surely claim his work was inspired by God, a new revelation for an open canon. But, as we realize, that claim makes no explicit impact on the Mishnah. And it would be some time before the canonical Gospels were given the standing of revelation through the Holy Spirit; it is a claim they do not make in their own behalf.

Fourth, at the very least, someone would link his opinions to biblical verses through the exegesis of the latter in line with the former so Scripture would validate his views. The authorship of the Mishnah did so only occasionally, but far more commonly stated on its own authority whatever rules it proposed to lay down. In this regard Matthew shows, for instance in Chapter Two, how this would have looked; much of Matthew's Gospel places into relationship prophetic teachings about the Messiah and the life, teachings, and actions of Jesus Christ.

The Hebrew of the Mishnah and of the other writings of the Oral Torah complicated the problem, because it is totally different from the Hebrew of the Hebrew Scriptures. Its verb, for instance, makes provision for more than completed or continuing action, for which the biblical Hebrew verb allows, but also for past and future times, subjunctive and indicative voices, and much else. The syntax is Indo-European, just as Latin and Greek are Indo-European languages, in that we can translate the word order of the Mishnah into any Indo-European language and come up with perfect sense. None of that crabbed imitation of biblical Hebrew, that makes the Dead Sea scrolls an embarrassment to read, characterizes the Hebrew of the Mishnah. Mishnaic style is elegant, subtle, exquisite in its sensitivity to word order and repetition, balance, pattern.

The solution to the problem of the authority of the Mishnah, that is to say, its relationship to Scripture, was worked out in the period after the closure of the Mishnah. Since no one now could credibly claim to sign the name of Ezra or Adam to a book of this kind, and since biblical Hebrew had provided no apologetic aesthetics whatever, the only options lay elsewhere. The two were to, first, provide a story of the origin of the contents of the Oral Torah, beginning with the Mishnah, and, second, link each allegation of the Oral Torah, again starting with the Mishnah, through processes of biblical (not mishnaic) exegesis, to verses of the Scriptures.

These two procedures, together, would establish for the Mishnah that standing that the uses to which the document was to be put demanded for it: a place in the canon of Israel, a legitimate relationship to the Torah of Moses. And with the notion that the Mishnah and later writings that amplified and explained its law formed a component of the Oral Torah, the writing down of the Oral Torah began. As people began to bring to the Written Torah, or Jewish Scriptures, the questions of amplification and explanation that they brought to the Mishnah, they wrote down the answers to their questions too. These accumulated and were collected and organized in the midrash compilations that we have reviewed in our reading of the biblical accounts of Creation, Adam, Noah, the Flood, Abraham, Isaac, Jacob, and the Ten Commandments. And that is how the Oral Torah came to be written down: the one-time occasion, but not the all-time contents.

The upshot is very simple. The founders of Judaism as we know it, who flourished in the first seven centuries of the Common Era, brought Scripture into their world, and their world into Scripture. They therefore show us how people shaped their understanding of the world out of the resources of God's revelation of the beginnings of humanity, and, especially, of God's people, Israel. The great sages, honored with the title of rabbi, transformed the Torah into a plan and design for the world, the everyday as an instance of the eternal. They read Scripture as God's picture of creation and humanity. They read the life of the streets and marketplaces, the home and the hearth, the nations and the world, as an ongoing commentary on Scripture and the potentialities (not all of them good) of creation. So as we now realize full well, Torah flows in both directions.

Part Five

CONTEMPORARY MESSAGES
AND THEIR MEDIA

9

Liturgy in Judaism: Why Some Rites Retain Power in the Case of Contemporary Judaism

The power of liturgy, including sacrament and prayer, forms the generative reality of Roman Catholic Christianity, which has from the very founding of the Eucharist discovered the life of the faith in the sacraments as the Church has handed on those sacraments, and then, only then, in the declaration of faith through theology or in the realization of faith through institutions of culture and politics. First came the liturgy, then the story, and long afterward, the theology. My question in this context, which is why some rites retain power and others do not, will perhaps present a dissonance. Do not all rites retain their supernatural force? From God's perspective they do. But from a worldly angle of vision, matters are otherwise. We Americans know that some rites retain enormous power over popular imagination and behavior, and, alas, others do not. A simple census of the number of Christians in Church on Christmas or Easter tells us that, for vast numbers, attending Church worship on those occasions carries greater weight than doing so on any other occasion.

I mean to raise a question concerning liturgy, therefore, that is not liturgical, but that helps us understand the power of liturgy in the world as we know it. It is in terms of Judaic religious life and practice today that I shall frame and answer my question – why this, not that. Why is it that some liturgies bear enormous power, and others find themselves neglected? The reason is not that Judaic religious life is weaker or stronger than the Roman Catholic or the Buddhist or the Muslim or the Protestant or Orthodox Christian. Nor is the reason that that life is attenuated. The simple reason is that the Jews live in a variety of worlds, Western here in Europe and in the USA, Middle

Eastern in the State of Israel. They form a bridge from one form of modern life to another. They furthermore are sufficiently familiar so that people can draw conclusions and generalizations from their particular case. But they are sufficiently different so that people can compare and contrast that case with others of a more numerous or representative sector of contemporary life. So we ask ourselves, in a general way, are there liturgies that enjoy greater popular adherence than others, and if so, what are they?

The answer depends upon recognition that not one but two Judaisms flourish in the West, and the liturgies of each reach deep into the hearts of Jews. The one Judaism is for home and family life, and it is the received Judaism of the Dual Torah, written and oral, or one of that Judaism's continuators. The other Judaism is for public and corporate life, and it is the civil religion of a different Judaism altogether, one that I call the Judaism of Holocaust and Redemption. So, in point of fact, there are two Judaisms that flourish in the vast middle range of the socially integrated Jewries of the West, one for home and family, one for the shared life of the corporate community. Each of these two Judaisms answers an urgent question, but the question for the one is not the same as that addressed by the other.

The Judaism found compelling in the private life derives from the Judaism of the Dual Torah, oral and written, that took shape in late antiquity, the first seven centuries of the Common Era, and reached its definitive statement in the Talmud of Babylonia. That Judaism not only flourished as the normative and paramount system into the nineteenth century, but now, on the eve of the twenty-first, continues to impart shape and structure to the ongoing life of the synagogue, its liturgy, its holy days and festivals, its theology, its way of life and worldview.

The second Judaism – the Judaism of Holocaust and Redemption, strongly identified with the rise of the State of Israel – came on the scene only in the aftermath of World War II and the rise of the State of Israel. I call it the "Judaism of Holocaust and Redemption" because it is a Judaic system that invokes, as its generative worldview, the catastrophe of the destruction by Germany of most of the Jews of Europe between 1933 and 1945 and the creation, three years afterward, of the State of Israel. This Judaism, too, has its way of life, its religious duties, its public celebrations. It is communal, stressing public policy and practical action. It involves political issues, for example, policy toward the State of Israel, government assistance in helping Soviet Jews gain freedom, and, in the homelands of the Jewish Americans or Canadians or Britons or French, matters of local politics as well.

The first of the two Judaisms flourishes in the synagogue, as I said, and the second, in the streets. The one is private, the other public, the one personal and familial, the other civic and communal. That other Judaism exercises the power to transform civic and public affairs in Jewry as much as the Judaism of the Dual Torah enchants and changes the personal and familial ones. In politics, history, in society, Jews in Europe and North America respond to the Judaism of the Holocaust and Redemption in such a way as to imagine they are someone else, living somewhere else, at another time and circumstance. That vision transforms families into an Israel, a community.

Let me now spell out one among the many rites of the individual and the family that liturgically evokes profound response among Jews. It is the Days of Awe, the New Year or Rosh Hashshanah, and the Day of Atonement, or Yom Hakkipurim. These days are nearly universally observed by Jews throughout the world. They are days of profound religious feeling and spirit; there is nothing national or particular about them; their themes are individual and also universal.

Called in America "the holy holy days," the Days of Awe, ten momentous days from Rosh Hashshanah, the New Year, through Yom Kippur, the Day of Atonement, fill the synagogues to overflowing. Bare empty space on Sabbaths and festivals, the synagogues on the Days of Awe set the stage for mob scenes. And that fact presents a puzzle. Clearly, Judaism does work its enchantment and transforms some moments – some, but not others. Since there are plenty of empty seats on the Sabbath between the New Year and the Day of Atonement, as on all other Sabbaths, it is not the season alone. The point is that the same Judaism, invoking the same symbolic system and mythic structure, in some instances transforms but in others changes nothing. If people respond to one rite and not another, we ask what makes one rite compelling, another irrelevant. To understand the way worlds come from words, we have to explain both what works and what does not.

We listen first to the answer, then recover the question, of the rite. It is the question that the rite answers that provides a key to the treasury of the spirit contained within that rite. Only having taken up the contents of the liturgy may we seek an explanation in the larger context of contemporary Judaism and so explain why this, not that. The same theory that tells us why people respond to one liturgy has also to explain why they do not respond to some other. When we can explain why this, not that, we shall have reached the end of our inquiry into the transformation that the received Judaism can, and cannot, accomplish. So to ask the question: what basic theory, framed in the heart and soul of the religious life of Judaism, will explain the popularity of the Passover Seder, which nearly everyone does, and the neglect of the Sabbath, which nearly no one does, and what moves people on Rosh Hashshanah but not on The Festival of Sukkot, following soon afterward?

First, let us listen with some care to the answers of the Days of Awe, for through these we shall find it possible to state the questions, from which, in our further step outward, we shall reach that larger social context that frames the whole. The New Year, Rosh Hashshanah, and the Day of Atonement, Yom Kippur, together mark days of solemn penitence, at the start of the autumn festival season. The words of the liturgy, specifically, create a world of personal introspection, individual judgment. The turning of the year marks a time of looking backward. It is melancholy, like the falling leaves, but hopeful: even as, in baseball, with the Pennant and the Series' losers: next year is another season.

The answer of the Days of Awe concerns life and death, which take mythic form in affirmations of God's rule and judgment. The words create a world aborning, the old now gone, the new just now arriving. The New Year, Rosh Hashshanah, celebrates the creation of the world: *Today the world was born.* The time of new beginnings also marks endings: *On the New Year the decree is issued: Who will live and who will die?* At the New Year – so the words state – humanity is inscribed for life or death in the heavenly books for the coming year, and on the Day of Atonement the books are sealed. The world comes out to hear these words. The season is rich in celebration. The synagogues on that day are filled – whether with penitents or people who merely wish to be there hardly matters. The New Year is a day of remembrance on which the deeds of all creatures are reviewed. The principal themes of the words invoke creation, and God's rule over creation, revelation, and God's rule in the Torah for the created world, and redemption, God's ultimate plan for the world.

On the birthday of the world God made, God asserts his sovereignty, as in the New Year Prayer:

> Our God and God of our Fathers, Rule over the whole world in Your honor...and appear in Your glorious might to all those who dwell in the civilization of Your world, so that everything made will know that You made it, and every creature discern that You have created him, so that all in whose nostrils is breath may say, 'The Lord, the God of Israel is king, and His kingdom extends over all.'

Liturgical words concerning divine sovereignty, divine memory, and divine disclosure correspond to creation, revelation, and redemption. Sovereignty is established by creation of the world. Judgment depends upon law: "From the beginning You made this, Your purpose known...."

And therefore, since people have been told what God requires of them, they are judged:

> On this day sentence is passed upon countries, which to the sword and which to peace, which to famine and which to plenty, and each creature is judged today for life or death. Who is not judged on this day? For the remembrance of every creature comes before You, each man's deeds and destiny, words and way.

These are strong words for people to hear. As life unfolds and people grow reflective, the Days of Awe seize the imagination: I live, I die, sooner or later it comes to all. The call for inner contemplation implicit in the mythic words elicits a deep response.

The most personal, solemn, and moving of the Days of Awe is the Day of Atonement, *Yom Kippur,* the Sabbath of Sabbaths. It is marked by fasting and continuous prayer. On it, the Jew makes confession:

> Our God and God of our fathers, may our prayer come before You. Do not hide yourself from our supplication, for we are not so arrogant or stiff-necked as to say before You....We are righteous and have not sinned. But we have sinned.
>
> We are guilt laden, we have been faithless, we have robbed....
>
> We have committed iniquity, caused unrighteousness, have been presumptuous....
>
> We have counseled evil, scoffed, revolted, blasphemed....

The Hebrew confession is built upon an alphabetical acrostic, as if by making certain every letter is represented, God, who knows human secrets, will combine them into appropriate words. The very alphabet bears witness against us before God. Prayers to be spoken by the congregation are all in the plural: "For the sin which we have sinned against You with the utterance of the lips....For the sin which we have sinned before You openly and secretly." The community takes upon itself responsibility for what is done in it. All Israel is part of one community, one body, and all are responsible for the acts of each. The sins confessed are mostly against society, against one's fellowmen; few pertain to ritual laws. At the end comes a final word:

> O my God, before I was formed, I was nothing. Now that I have been formed, it is as though I had not been formed, for I am dust in my life, more so after death. Behold I am before You like a vessel filled with shame and confusion. May it be Your will...that I may no more sin, and forgive the sins I have already committed in Your abundant compassion.

While much of the liturgy speaks of "we," the individual focus dominates, beginning to end.

The Days of Awe speak to the heart of the individual, telling a story of judgment and atonement. So the individual Jew stands before God: possessing no merits, yet hopeful of God's love and compassion. If that is the answer, can there be any doubt about the question? The power of the Days of Awe derives from the sentiments and emotions aroused by the theme of those days: what is happening to me? Where am I going? Moments of introspection and reflection serve as guideposts in people's lives. That is why people treasure such moments and respond to the opportunities that define them. The themes of the Days of Awe stated in mythic terms address the human condition, and the message penetrates to the core of human concerns about life and death, the year past, the year beyond, the wrongs and the sins and the remissions and atonement. People nearly universally respond to the liturgy of sin and confession, atonement and forgiveness. But the same people on the next Sabbath rarely find their way to that same synagogue that they crowded on the Days of Awe.

The issue of the power of one liturgy, not some other, derives neither from faith nor doubt. The same people who pray the words I have quoted neglect other words of equal power within Judaism. If the issue is not that the more reasonable is the more practiced, then what explains the power of some words and not others? In my view, the issue is the question and the answer – people will believe all sorts of things if they want to, and deny the end of their nose if they do not want to. The rites of the actually practiced Judaism, denoted by the words that create worlds, have in common a single trait: it is their focus on the individual, inclusive of the family. The rites of the Judaism that for the generality of Jewry do not work to make worlds exhibit this common trait: they speak to a whole society, or to civilization, to nation or people. The corporate community, doing things together and all at once, conducts worship as service. The corporate community celebrates and commemorates events in the world of creation, revelation, and redemption. Sabbaths and festivals focus upon the corporate life of Israel, a social entity. The words that people say on these occasions do not speak to many Jews. The individual rites of passage, celebrating family, such as circumcision, marriage, and the rites that focus upon the individual and his or her existence, such as the Days of Awe, retain enormous power to move people.

The liturgies of the Sabbath and festivals are neglected. Why is that so? Because they present powerful answers to questions people do not want to ask in the synagogue, but do ask elsewhere. Why this, not that? I point to the message contained in the rites that speak to the subjectivity and individuality of circumstance, lay stress on the private person, recognize and accord priority to the autonomous and autocephalic individual. What people find personally relevant they accept; for them, the words evoke meaning and make worlds. The rites that speak to the community out there beyond family, to the corporate existence of people who see themselves as part of a social entity beyond, scarcely resonate. The context, therefore, accounts for the difference and even for variations. Jews live one by one, family by family. Words that speak to that individuality work wonders. Jews do not form a corporate community but only families. Words that address the commonality of Israel not as the congregation of individual Jews but as a community bound by law to do some things together, fall unheard, mere magic, not wonder-working at all.

To state the upshot in secular terms, the fundamental condition of "being Jewish" so far as people identify "being Jewish" with the received Judaism of the Dual Torah in the West is that it involves individual and family, *but imparts in social experience no knowledge of what it means to live in corporate community.* People cannot appeal to experience of a life in Israel and as Israel, an entire social entity, so as to validate the issues resolved by the rites of the corporate community, the Sabbath, for example, and the synagogue. The questions of community are not asked, not felt, not understood, so the answers in rite give information no one needs or can use.

Now that we have begun to form a theory of where and why words work and do not work, we confront the single most puzzling fact in contemporary Judaism. It is the contrast between the vivid and encompassing life of the faith in families, and the decadent state of the synagogue in its critical function, of the offering up of prayer day by day and on Sabbaths and festivals. The simple fact that families covering nearly the whole of American Israel celebrate the Passover banquet Seder but only paltry numbers then assemble the next morning in synagogue worship states the question. The fact that nearly all Jews bury their deceased in accord with the rites of Judaism (whether Reform or Orthodox) underlines the question. Why the one, not the other?

The reason is simple. Public worship rests upon the experience of the corporate community, which is responsible *in the aggregate* for offering up prayers. But so far as Jews as a whole confess to a common experience of the world, it bears no relationship to worship or the responsibilities of divine service. So, once more, what we see is the transformation of Judaism into an exercise, by choice, of home and family, rather than an expression, out of duty imposed from above and beyond, of the corporate community, Israel, God's people. People who do not in their ordinary life experience the commonality of community also do not, in their cultic life, conceive that a task awaits for which all bear responsibility, and to which the personal attitudes and feelings of the individual prove immaterial.

The conception of prayer characteristic of the Judaism of the Dual Torah that took shape in the first six centuries of the Common Era and predominated until now derives from the Temple and its priesthood and offerings. Prayer, that Judaism held, continues the offerings of the altar to God. Now the priesthood in the book of Leviticus represented those offerings in a very particular way, and that representation predominates in the Mishnah, ca. 200, and its exegetical continuations in the Tosefta, the Talmud of the Land of Israel, and the Talmud of Babylonia, ca. 300-600. In these definitive documents, the priestly conception of the Temple cult shaped the synagogue activity of prayer. That conception treated the offerings of the altar in the Temple in Jerusalem (the "tent of meeting" of the books of Exodus, Leviticus, and Numbers) as responses to God's command: This you shall do. The language is simple: "The Lord spoke to Moses saying, Speak to the children of Israel and say to them...." The command addressed the community as a whole through the priesthood.

People with no knowledge of a religious life lived out in corporate society, who see religion as, if not utterly personal, then fundamentally familial, can hardly expect themselves to recognize obligations to offer up, as a group, the recitation of certain words. The issue is not that offering up unfelt words taxes the imagination, while offering up compelling words makes sense. The same social experience that tells us why the vast majority of Jews form families to observe the Passover banquet rite explains why they do not ordinarily participate in public worship in the synagogue. Their social experience informs them that under the aspect of eternity to be a Jew is to be part of a family, but tells them little in the aspect of their inner life about corporate responsibilities as a community.

So let me give my answer to the question, why this, not that. Some liturgies change us, others do not, because some words refer to worlds we know, others speak of things we cannot recognize or identify. The individual in family understands life as metaphor. The family as part of community within the realm of religion does not. Corporate Israel exists in other dimensions, but not in the religious one. Consequently, the synagogue, which has served the very specific purpose of divine service to God through both the provision of public worship as is required of the community and the study of the Torah in public as is also demanded of the community, both changes and decays. It changes into a community center, flourishing (where it does) in those aspects of its program to which the holy words scarcely reach. It decays in that the service of the heart becomes lip-service, words passively mumbled in suppression of utter incredulity.

Now, Jews' understanding religion as essentially private and personal, this is a generation of home and family to which supernatural collectivities such as holy Israel, a corporate community before God, have little appeal. Experiences in life that everyone has, such as hunger and satisfaction, having a baby, feeling different, or getting married undergo transformation because, to begin with, they refer to facts of life that are very real to us. But to what shared experience does public worship appeal, beyond an obligation to say the prayers? For Jews as for others in American and European Protestant societies, religion is personal. What forms families into communities are experiences of a different order altogether. They therefore invoke a different set of metaphors from those they conceive to be religious. These other metaphors interpret corporate experience in what are deemed appropriate, therefore essentially political, terms. And their liturgies play a powerful role as well. But it is a different set of liturgies, deriving from a different Judaism, from the one that speaks of God's revelation to Moses at Mount Sinai.

Jews form a corporate community and share a substantial range of social experience. But that shared social experience in politics also takes form in transformations of the given into a gift, so that the *is* of the everyday polity shades into the *as if* of another time and place, as much as in the transformation by the Judaism of the Dual Torah of the passage of the individual through the cycle of life. The social experience forms the premise of the religious life. But the Jews' social experience of polity and community does not match the religious experience of home and family. Hence the religious side to things conforms to the boundaries of family, and the public experience of politics, economics, and society that Jews share comes to expression in quite different ways altogether.

The other Judaism, the one of Holocaust and Redemption rather than Eden, Sinai, and the World to Come, is political in its themes and character, myth and rites. The worldview of the Judaism of Holocaust and Redemption evokes political, historical events – the destruction of the Jews in Europe, the creation of the state of Israel, two events of a wholly political character. It treats these events as unique, just as the Judaism of the Dual Torah treats Eden and Adam's fall, Sinai, and the coming redemption, as unique. It finds in these events the ultimate meaning of the life of the Jews together as Israel, and it therefore defines an Israel for itself – the State of Israel in particular – just as the Judaism of the Dual Torah finds in Eden, Sinai, and the world to come the meaning of the life of Israel and so defines for itself an Israel too:

the holy Israel, the social entity different in its very essence from all other social entities. That other Judaism, the Judaism of Holocaust and Redemption, addresses the issues of politics and public policy that Jews take up in their collective social activity. But it, too, has its rites and even its liturgies.

When we ask why the bifurcation between the personal and the familial, subjected to the Judaism of the Dual Torah, perceived as religion, and the public and civic, governed by the Judaism of Holocaust and Redemption, perceived as politics, we turn outward. For the explanation lies in the definition of permissible difference in North America and the place of religion in that difference. Specifically, in North American society, defined as it is by Protestant conceptions, it is permissible to be different in religion, and religion is a matter of what is personal and private. Hence Judaism as a religion encompasses what is personal and familial. The Jews as a political entity then put forth a separate system, one that concerns not religion, which is not supposed to intervene in political action, but public policy. Judaism in public policy produces political action in favor of the State of Israel, or Soviet Jewry, or other important matters of the corporate community.

Judaism in private affects the individual and the family and is not supposed to play a role in politics at all. That pattern conforms to the Protestant model of religion, and the Jews have accomplished conformity to it by the formation of two Judaisms. A consideration of the Protestant pattern, which separates not the institutions of Church from the activities of the state, but the entire public polity from the inner life, will show us how to make sense of the presence of the two Judaisms of North America and in much of Europe as well. I see the reason in a simple misunderstanding of the nature of religion. In Protestant North America, people commonly see religion as something personal and private, prayer, for example, therefore speaks for the individual. No wonder, then, that those enchanted words and gestures that, for their part, Jews adopt, transform the inner life, recognize life's transitions, and turn them into rites of passage. It is part of a larger prejudice that religion and rite speak to the heart of the particular person. What can be changed by rite, then, is primarily personal and private, not social, not an issue of culture, not effective in politics, not part of the public interest.

Liturgy is an act not of sociology but of faith. Still, we who carry out the liturgy live in society and form our religious imagination in the crucible of the here and the now. It is no wonder, then, that, for contemporary Judaism, a religion that is personal and familiar should compete with a religion that is public and corporate. For, in the life of Jews as of Christians and Muslims and Buddhists and others, that is how we receive and live life in this day. Since the life of society is marked by difference, all of us have to find space within our lives for being of more than a single order. And our social experience comes prior to our religious vocation. True, in religion, God made the world. But the religious community – in this case, Israel, the holy people of God – is what consecrates the world. The words of religion – liturgies – do not make religion. Religious people make religion. And, like the builders of the tower of Babel, all they have for mortar is slime.

10

The Historical Medium
for the Theological Message

Arno J. Mayer, *Why Did the Heavens Not Darken? The "Final Solution" in History.* New York: Pantheon Books, 1988. 492 pp. $27.95

Charles S. Maier, *The Unmasterable Past. History, Holocaust, and German National Identity.* Cambridge: Harvard University Press, 1988. 227 pp. $22.50

These two books are brilliant, profound, important, but utterly irrelevant. They ask a question deriving from contemporary politics in their address to events of the past, and the answers have no bearing whatever upon the events of which they speak, but only concern how we see things. It is hard to imagine a field of learning so askew as historical study today, which studies what was to tell us not what happened or even to purport to explain what now is, but what should be. Historical positivism here lays claim to settle questions not of fact but of value, purpose, meaning. And that intellectual enterprise is bankrupt. Let me explain.

Two historians of modern Europe, both of them at the senior ranks of the historical profession, here undertake that kind of rethinking of historical paradigms people know as revisionism. Each asks a fresh question of familiar facts. The upshot is to direct our attention to facts not earlier seen as important, to reshape our understanding of the past. So far so good. But, when we see what is at stake, we perceive a deeper issue, and it is not a historical one at all.

In rethinking the destruction of most of the Jews of continental Europe between 1933 and 1945, now recast into a symbol for which the word "The Holocaust," stands, both historians address the contemporary sensibility. The question they ask derives, therefore, not so much from the events as from the received interpretation of the events under description. People generally view the murder of the Jews of Europe as integral to the Nazi platform from the beginning. Mayer distinguishes their virulent anti-Semitism from genocide. More to the point, he sees that genocide in the larger setting of European history. It is no longer, as is claimed, "unique," but enjoys analogies. Similar circumstances produced similar events. Maier for his part addresses the canonical claim that "The Holocaust" was unique, understanding that the claim itself serves acutely contemporary purposes of policy and polemic.

Both scholars originate in European Jewish families, and both rehearse their own connections to the subject at hand. Each writes with vigor and force; the two books form contemporary classics of historical writing. And neither presents a thesis that we may dismiss as trivial or inconsequential.

Mayer's is in three parts. First, "Nazi Germany's dual resolve to acquire living space in the east and liquidate the Soviet regime provided the essential geopolitical, military, and ideological preconditions for the Judeocide." Second, the catastrophe is to be seen in the historical context of its time: the Bolshevik revolution in Russia, the Nazi counterrevolution in Germany. Third, the Nazi regime, the eastern campaign, the Judeocide, form "integral components and expressions of the General Crisis and Thirty Years War of the twentieth century." So to the conclusion: "Nazi Germany experienced an irreversible increase of entropy in its civil and political society while fighting a life-or-death struggle with Soviet Russia, despoiling most of the Continent, and visiting its vengeful fury on European Jewry."

How does Mayer's thesis fall into the classification of "revisionism"? Here is where historical study fades over into theological advocacy. The mass murder of the Jews is not unique, parachuted down onto the space of earth, but stands in relationship to "the singular historical context in which it was conceived and executed." Then "The Holocaust" cannot be deemed unique. Not only so, but the mass murder was not inevitable; it does not then attest to the character of "human nature," or "all of us," nor do we deal with evidence concerning the divine "hiding of the face" or "tremendum." Judeocide was not inevitable. The original intent was to deport the Jews. Mayer argues, "As long as the Wehrmact...[was] triumphant, the suffering of the Jews was limited to this victimization by German security forces and local collaborationist vigilantes. This essentially unsystematic killing of Jews coincided with the expectation of a quick victory over the Red Army." The mass murder, of a systematic character, was precipitated by the failure of the eastern campaign:

"Hitler's ideologically and politically grounded decision to turn the failing war-cum-crusade against Soviet Russia and bolshevism into a ferocious struggle for *Sein oder Nichtsein* (life or death) entailed the pitiless torment of the Jews." And again, "The Judeocide erupted and was systematized in this context of monstrous death and destruction, and it was carried out in a setting and atmosphere weighted down with the miseries of war...The main body of European Jewry was forced to endure torments of another order entirely."

The revisionism enters in when Mayer turns to the uses of history:

> This cult of remembrance [of The Holocaust] has become overly sectarian. More and more, it has helped to disconnect the Jewish catastrophe from its secular historical setting, while placing it within the providential history of the Jewish people to be commemorated, lamented, and restrictively interpreted. Its reification has found expression and consecration in the religiously freighted word concept 'the Holocaust,' a term whose standard meaning is a sacrificial offering wholly consumed by fire in exaltation of God.

Here is the connection between the facts of history and the quest for meaning: the uses of the past for contemporary debate. The premise, of course, accounts for the appeal of historical study. Events not only instruct, they also impose judgment, and we may settle theological questions by appeal to material facts.

That is the point at which Maier's work proves relevant to German debates concerning comparability of events, with the explicit concern about whether one atrocity is like another and whether any can be deemed unique. For these debates concern not the interpretation of the dead past, but the shaping of the present and future of German politics and culture. This is not historical study but philosophical advocacy, again, theology in a secular mode. Maier, in tracing these matters, reflects on how historical study (not "history") shapes national identity and collective responsibility. Maier moves outward from the German historians' conflict concerning whether the Nazi crimes were unique or comparable to other crimes. He concedes, "Comparability cannot really exculpate." But, he admits, "uniqueness is rightly perceived as a crucial issue." Why does it matter to Germans? Because, "If the Final Solution remains non-comparable...the past may never be 'worked through,' the future never normalized, and German nationhood may remain forever tainted, like some well forever poisoned." Quite how all this follows I cannot explain, but, Maier amply demonstrates, that is precisely what is at issue in the Germany he so ably described. That at stake is contemporary, not historical, politics is shown by the framing of the issue. Jürgen Habermas sees the claim that the German destruction of European Jewry finds its place within the range of other genocides as an effort to "relativize" the event, and this he places within a new nationalist and conservative search for a usable past. Accordingly, as Maier sets forth, "all participants have recognized that there can be no discussion of a national community without a confrontation of the darkest aspects of the national past." So "the controversy is also about the German future."

The voice is the voice of Jacob, but the hands are the hands of Esau. Both books – absolutely first-rate pieces of historical writing, compelling reading, important learning, true vindications of the historians' craft – therefore put forth the hands of history but they speak in the voice of policy concerning tomorrow. Neither one can have been written if the author's sole interest lay in what happened then; nor is the meaning of events permitted to reside mainly in the past. But then we have to ask ourselves, *cui bono*? In a very profound sense, so what? Mayer's brilliant and, I think, completely successful revision of our understanding of the place of the Judeocide in European history helps us better to understand what happened. But it bears no moral authority concerning what we are to make of what happened. The facts of history lie inert, and they cannot be made to live simply because they are set upon the stage of contemporary debate. For facts are just that: dead. They bear no meaning, contain no moral authority, that for our own purposes we do not impute to them. To the millions who lie in the dust, to the millions more, myself included, who suffer every day with the pain of memory, all of these debates, as they address issues not of fact and analysis but of contemporary interpretation of tomorrow's imperatives, are in an exact sense irrelevant.

Where have we learned to appeal to facts of history to settle issues of faith and value? It is from the tradition of nineteenth-century German historicism, which took the view that if we know exactly what was, we can also say what should be. But the connection between the was and the should be hardly emerges from any logic intrinsic in inert facts. And those facts that we identify as important gain consequence only because we give it to them. The debates Maier records, the events Mayer traces, bear no implications out of the past concerning an inchoate future. The future is what, in our conscience and intellect, we decide it should be. History has now to leave the stage of theology and philosophy alike; it has nothing relevant to say to the things that matter. Facts do not settle questions of faith because faith is not something that the here and the now dictates.

Index

Aaron 138

Abba Saul 125

Abigail 11

Abraham 29, 51, 145

Acts 115, 120, 123, 125, 153

Adam 84, 144, 145

altar 42, 84, 91, 117, 130-132, 156

analogical-contrastive reasoning 63, 65

Antigonus of Sokho 137, 141

Aramaic 138, 139

Aristotle, Aristotelian 9, 58-61, 68, 69, 79-81, 87-89, 97, 98, 100

atonement 10, 37, 38, 41, 84, 128, 151-154

Augustine 68, 79, 98

Avery-Peck, Alan J. 127-129

Avtalyon 138

Babylonia 36, 72, 93, 150, 156

Baruch 144

blood 118, 130-132

Brooks, Roger 120, 121

Buddhist 149

burnt-offering 41-43

canon 4, 7, 14, 20, 22, 37, 58, 144, 145

Christ 68, 141, 144, 145

Christian(s) 68, 75, 78, 79, 98, 140, 149

Christianity, Christianities 68, 69, 78, 79, 98, 143, 149

Constantine 78

creation 44, 73, 90, 91, 110, 144-146, 150, 152, 154, 157

David 10, 11

Day of Atonement 37, 38, 151-153

Days of Awe 151-154

Dead Sea 4, 15, 19

Dead Sea Scrolls 145

Deuteronomy (Dt., Deut.) 10, 11, 29, 31, 51, 72

divorce 60, 112, 113

Dual Torah 7, 13, 58-61, 67, 68, 150, 151, 155-158

economics 59, 67-77, 82, 89, 90, 97, 98, 157

Eden 28, 84, 90, 157

Eduyyot 38, 49, 101

Egypt 36

Eilberg-Schwartz, Howard 102-104, 106, 115

Eleazar ben Arakh 142

Brown Judaic Studies

140167	*The Legacy of Hermann Cohen*	William Kluback
140168	*Method and Meaning in Ancient Judaism*	Jacob Neusner
140169	*The Role of the Messenger and Message in the Ancient Near East*	
		John T. Greene
140171	*Abraham Heschel's Idea of Revelation*	Lawerence Perlman
140172	*The Philosophical Mishnah Volume IV: The Repertoire*	Jacob Neusner
140173	*From Ancient Israel to Modern Judaism Volume 2: Intellect in Quest of Understanding*	Neusner/Frerichs/Sarna
140174	*From Ancient Israel to Modern Judaism Volume 3: Intellect in Quest of Understanding*	Neusner/Frerichs/Sarna
140175	*From Ancient Israel to Modern Judaism Volume 4: Intellect in Quest of Understanding*	Neusner/Frerichs/Sarna
140176	*Translating the Classics of Judaism: In Theory and In Practice*	Jacob Neusner
140177	*Profiles of a Rabbi: Synoptic Opportunities in Reading About Jesus*	
		Bruce Chilton
140178	*Studies in Islamic and Judaic Traditions II*	William Brinner/Stephen Ricks

Brown Studies on Jews and Their Societies

145001	*American Jewish Fertility*	Calvin Goldscheider
145003	*The American Jewish Community*	Calvin Goldscheider
145004	*The Naturalized Jews of the Grand Duchy of Posen in 1834 and 1835*	Edward David Luft
145005	*Suburban Communities: The Jewishness of American Reform Jews*	Gerald L. Showstack
145007	*Ethnic Survival in America*	David Schoem

Brown Studies in Religion

147001	*Religious Writings and Religious Systems Volume 1*	Jacob Neusner, et al
147002	*Religious Writings and Religious Systems Volume 2*	Jacob Neusner, et al
147003	*Religion and the Social Sciences*	Robert Segal